WINNING
with
TRUST
in
BUSINESS

WINNING
with
TRUST
in
BUSINESS

ARTHUR H. BELL AND RICHARD G. COHN

PELICAN PUBLISHING COMPANY
GRETNA 2008

*With love to my mother, Dorothy,
in celebration of her ninetieth birthday*
—A. B.

*To my wife, Anne, and my children, Ryan and Grace,
for their loving support and enduring patience*
—R. G. C.

Copyright © 2008
By Arthur H. Bell and Richard G. Cohn
All rights reserved

*The word "Pelican" and the depiction of a pelican are trademarks
of Pelican Publishing Company, Inc., and are registered in the
U.S. Patent and Trademark Office.*

Library of Congress Cataloging-in-Publication Data

Bell, Arthur H. (Arthur Henry), 1946-
  Winning with trust in business / Arthur H. Bell and Richard G. Cohn.
     p. cm.
  ISBN 978-1-58980-380-0 (hardcover : alk. paper) 1. Organizational behavior—United States. 2. Trust. 3. Communication in organizations—United States. 4. Work environment—United States. I. Cohn, Richard G. II. Title.
  HD58.7.B447 2008
  658.4—dc22
                           2008018821

*The diagnostic instrument included in Appendix A is based on the evaluation
published in* Winning with Difficult People, *third edition (Barron's Educational
Series, copyright 2003), by Arthur H. Bell and Dayle M. Smith. Reprinted by
arrangement with Barron's Educational Series, Hauppauge, New York.
Research in Chapter 9 draws in part upon Arthur Bell's* Preparing for
Intercultural Business Opportunity, *copyright Arthur Bell, 1999.*

Printed in the United States of America
Published by Pelican Publishing Company, Inc.
1000 Burmaster Street, Gretna, Louisiana 70053

*To the millions of workers building trust in
one another and in their leaders*

Contents

	Acknowledgments 9
Chapter One	An Overview of Workplace Trust 13
Chapter Two	Building Organizational Trust 21
Chapter Three	Individual Trust and Candor in the Workplace 39
Chapter Four	The Corrupting Influence of a Lack of Trust 51
Chapter Five	Common Trust Busters at Work 83
Chapter Six	Struggles for Trust: The Personal Dimension 95
Chapter Seven	Building Individual Trust in the Workplace 123
Chapter Eight	Trust for the New Workforce 135
Chapter Nine	Trust in Global Business 155
Chapter Ten	Measuring Dimensions of Workplace Trust 175
Chapter Eleven	Conclusion 197
Appendix A	Trust and Personality: A Diagnostic Instrument 203
Appendix B	Recommended Readings 219

Acknowledgments

The authors gratefully acknowledge corporate leaders, executives, managers, and employees who have contributed their stories, experiences, and perspectives on the issue of trust in the workplace. We thank those individuals for their insights. Art Bell thanks Dean Mike Duffy, Associate Dean Zhan Li, and his colleagues at the Masagung Graduate School of Management, University of San Francisco, and the Naval Postgraduate School as well as his former colleagues at Georgetown University and the University of Southern California for their encouragement. In addition he would like to recognize friends and faculty at Harvard University for their willingness to discuss and debate a wide range of workplace issues and controversies. Special thanks go to our talented research assistant, Samie Miro Carter-Oberstone. Finally, the authors express sincere thanks to Nina Kooij, Lindsey Reynolds, Katie Szadziewicz, and their associates at Pelican Publishing Company for their dedication and expertise.

WINNING with TRUST in BUSINESS

Chapter One

An Overview of Workplace Trust

"Trust equity goes deeper than either brand equity or corporate image: it refers to the quality and quantity of trust that an organization or group enjoys. Both concrete and measurable, it is also critical to business success."

Daniel Yankelovich, author, researcher, and
leading analyst of business and social trends

This book is about trust in the workplace. We look at why so many workers across so many industries do not believe or trust their company's leaders. We explore the billions of dollars in economic loss and missed business opportunities resulting from a lack of accurate information and openness flowing through businesses today. However, this book is not about the moral, ethical, or even spiritual implications of telling the truth. This book is about the enormous economic value of candor in the workplace. It is about how candor and openness in the workplace strengthen competitiveness, organizational agility, and profitability of businesses.

An epidemic of spin, obfuscation, misinformation, and outright lying is taking place in companies of all sizes. This lack of candor threatens the viability of businesses everywhere, especially in the United States with its expanding service sector and knowledge-worker-based economy increasingly dependent on timely and accurate flows of information. We examine the impact on business and industry that occurs when less than half of American workers trust their CEOs and bosses. We also look at why so many workers do not openly express their views or make suggestions in the workplace or pass along customer complaints.

We are writing this book because too many American businesses are squandering their competitiveness and limiting their profits by maintaining low levels of trust within their workplaces. Too many company leaders treat candor and openness like options on a menu: candor is fine to sample sometimes, but more often they would prefer to try deception. On too many occasions where no legal or competitive reason exists, the truth is filtered, delayed, or obscured. Too many CEOs feel it is part of their job to put the company's best foot forward, even if it means misleading large segments of their workforce.

This book does not focus on the scores of American companies who extinguish trust with customers seeking assistance who face telephone labyrinths, online help desks, FAQs that no one ever asks, and untrained workers at telephone service centers. Instead, we focus on business leaders whose open-door policy extends mainly to yes-men and -women or who treat workers who have the guts to criticize a company decision as outcasts. We see too many ghost writers penning executives' words on internal company blogs. We see too many company publications and presentations to workers devoid of useable information. We continue to be shocked at the number of companies who do not offer any communications training to its managers at any time in their careers. We see so much spin in some companies' formal communications channels that many employees now rely almost exclusively on coworkers and informal communications networks for information to do their job.

We are also writing this book because it is time for workers to step up and play their role in establishing higher levels of trust and candor in the workplace. Too many employees do not pass along customer complaints or point out weaknesses or defects. Too many workers expect the company to take care of all their information needs, even in this Digital Information

A Failing Report Card for Trust in American Corporations

In a 2007 Towers Perrin survey of 25,000 employees, "the study found that almost half of all employees do not believe their leadership communicates effectively with them. Not surprisingly, the survey found that the organizations who received the highest marks for open and honest communication were those who were adept at delivering both good and bad news. These were the companies most likely to win the trust of their people."
Ken Lehman, Winning Workplaces

"The trust gap between consumers and corporations: Sixty-eight percent of executives say that large corporations have a generally or somewhat positive contribution to the public good. Yet only 48 percent of consumers agree."
Sheila Bonini, *The McKinsey Quarterly*, 2007

"The Better Business Bureau/Gallup Trust in Business Index survey found that nearly one in five (18 percent) adult American consumers say their trust in businesses that they regularly deal with has decreased in the past 12 months, more than twice as many who say their trust increased (8 percent). The survey also found that less than half of American consumers (49 percent) say they have a great deal (12 percent) or quite a lot (37 percent) of trust in businesses that they regularly deal with."
Better Business Bureau, October 25, 2007

"Even while society's expectations are rising, its trust in multinational corporations is hitting new lows. In a 2006 McKinsey global survey of more than 4,000 consumers, only 33 percent of Europeans and 40 percent of Americans said they believed large, global companies act in the best interest of society at least some of the time. Yet winning or retaining people's trust is key to the success of any business. As the CEO of a large financial institution put it, '"The predominant concern for us is the erosion of trust, [which] is impacting our employee and customer franchises.'"
McKinsey UN Global Compact CEO
Participant Survey 2007

Age. Too many workers go along with unrealistic work plans or schedules because it is easier not to confront the miscalculations. Too many workers show up at presentations or town hall meetings with company executives and fail to ask the tough questions to their leaders.

The combination of company executives withholding and shading key information and employees not able or willing to speak up about problems directly threatens the financial vitality of companies. Survey after survey shows that at least half of the workforce does not trust their senior executives. Product ideas would circulate quicker, cross-organizational collaboration would increase, and new products would make it to market more rapidly with just a 10 percent increase in workplace trust. As large companies, especially American companies, become populated with more knowledge workers, we anticipate greater need for accurate and timely information flowing throughout the workforce.

Spin, commonly defined as placing the most positive light on news to manipulate its meaning, has migrated from the political arena to the business world. Just like politicians in Washington, most business executives do not write their own speeches. Similar to politicians parrying with reporters over election predictions or controversial issues, businesses play an extraordinary cat and mouse game with financial analysts and business reporters to make sure that quarterly financial results meet or exceed Wall Street's expectations. Too often, company leaders try to manipulate the flow of information on a business activity in distress instead of fostering a robust exchange of information and ideas within the workforce that may provide new insights and approaches. In a survey for Towers Perrin, conducted in 2003 by Harris Interactive of 1,000 working Americans from a broad range of industries and demographics, 55 percent of employees surveyed felt, "My company tries too hard to put a positive spin on issues in its communications to employees."

As technology levels the playing field for access to information, attempts at manipulating information directed at employees too often end up damaging the credibility of the company's leaders. Companies that manipulate communications with their employees clearly pay a "spin tax." Spinning employees with overly optimistic assessments of company decisions or failing to inform employees of impending troubles costs companies real money in terms of higher attrition and squandered business opportunities. Preoccupation by senior management with extolling its own virtues or pointing out its inventiveness shuts off the flow of new ideas and critical information from employees. The sanctity of many executive suites signals a distrust of others and their ideas. Employees numbed by corporate spin often do not pass along customer complaints, preventing the company from quickly rectifying a costly production error. Workers do not stop thinking about new and better ways of working or serving customers; they just stop passing their thoughts along when the communications arteries of a company are clogged with spin.

This book examines the impact of trust or the lack of trust on the workplace. Specifically, we will look at trust at the organization or corporate level and at the individual employee level. We use the term "candor" to describe the open and accurate exchange of information and ideas. We define "workplace trust" as the ability of different people and parts of a company to rely consistently on one another. We use the term "workplace" in a very broad sense to describe today's physical work environment, stretching from the factory floor, distribution center, and corporate headquarters to the inventor's garage and the corner store. "Workplace" also encompasses the array of online and digital technology that enables such "virtual" communications tools as videoconferencing, telecommuting, e-mail, online order processing, Web sites, cell phones, and laptop computers. We recognize that successful businesses are the result of the interplay of many factors and openly admit that this book focuses primarily on trust in the workplace.

We look at how companies reach the point where so many of

their employees and customers do not believe or trust their CEO. For some companies, we will find a tipping point where a steady stream of obfuscations, omissions, and misleading statements culminates in a loss of credibility. For other companies, we will discover a turning point, where in a critical situation facing the company—such as a layoff or product recall—its leaders take the path of shading rather than sharing the truth, and in so doing, destroy the bonds of trust within the workplace.

Companies combat pressures for quick results or increased transparency with an array of public relations strategies to get their story out and reassure customers and investors. Employees and customers often do not know who or what to believe as corporate spin, the rumor mill, and inaccurate reporting converge to cloud their understanding of the company and its business. We continue to see executives and managers delivering carefully crafted messages to their own workers with the intent to cover up corporate shortcomings in the mistaken view that what employees don't know won't hurt or distract them.

This book is written as a guide for the thousands of businesses losing employees, stifling innovation, frustrating customers, and squeezing profits because they do not talk straight. We take a hard look at companies cutting off new ideas or constructive criticism that may result in innovation and new products and services. We think employees have the responsibility in today's workplace to seek information on doing their jobs and serving customers. We also take on CEOs and others company leaders whose obfuscations, prevarications, and half-truths to the workforce destroy employee loyalty, increase turnover of key contributors, and sustain a culture of withholding rather than sharing information. We focus on managers and front-line employees trying to climb the corporate ladder by not rocking the corporate boat with honest criticism and new ideas. We challenge employees for going along with managers, executives, and CEOs who consistently treat employees as interchangeable economic units instead of a company's first contact with customers or the fountain of innovation keeping a company ahead of its competitors.

We examine communications technology to determine if information clutter is merely an unfortunate byproduct of removing time and distance as communications barriers. Or, does information overload—created by the proliferation of Web sites, e-mail, voice mail, cell phones, blogs, and podcasting—undermine the open and frank exchange of information and ideas necessary for an organization and its people to learn, collaborate, and innovate? We look at how globalization of supply chains, workforces, and customer bases removes the human face from multitudes of personal interactions that build relationships and trust. We delve into the paradox of a steep decline in workplace candor accompanying the avalanche of information now available in the workplace due largely to advances in computer technology. However, the reader will not find us lamenting the good old days of top-down communication where phrases like "command and control" defined best practices in management. We embrace the economy of the twenty-first century with its globalization of production, markets, and talent. We applaud the advances in technology that remove time, distance, and location as barriers to communications and commerce.

We offer a framework for companies to reestablish trust in the workplace. We help companies locate within their workplace where diminishing candor and openness actually hinder business processes or frustrate employees. We help companies identify managers who are making a difference with candor and openness. And, we show how employees from the factory floor and call center to the executive boardroom produce better business results with accurate and timely information. We offer solutions to unclogging communication bottlenecks caused by low levels of workplace trust. We share our views on corporate cultures and how these collective conversations often determine the capacity of a company and its people to work together and succeed in a highly competitive environment.

Please note that we do not dwell on criminal fabricators like Enron and the moral virtues of telling the truth. Instead of preaching, we hope to engage business leaders, managers, and workers in creating and benefiting from an open workplace with a robust and frank exchange of information and ideas. We do not plan on naming specific companies or leaders because we do not want this book to become a list of winners and losers in the corporate candor competition. Also, this book does not call for, in any way, a company to disclose competitive or proprietary information that would hamper its competitiveness.

We are writing this book to get American companies to do something about the lack of trust increasingly derailing innovation, driving away customers, and extinguishing loyalty among employees. We invite you to join us in building companies with free-flowing and accurate streams of information and ideas that will not only be more profitable but also better equipped to navigate economic cycles, business downturns, and global competition.

Chapter Two

Building Organizational Trust

"The real economic value of a corporation increasingly comes not from the assets that it owns, or the employees that it supervises, but from the domain of trust that it has established."
The Economist, *December 20, 2001*

By any reliable measure, low levels of workplace trust continue to hamper businesses of all sizes. Towers Perrin, a leading professional services firm specializing in organizational development and human resources, released its Global Workforce Study in the fall of 2007 based on a survey of nearly ninety thousand workers in eighteen countries. Only 38 percent of employees surveyed felt "senior management communicates openly and honestly." In other words, far less than half of employees across the globe trust senior management to talk straight with workers. Nearly one in five workers admit to telling lies at the office at least once a week, according to a 2005 survey of more than 2,000 workers by CareerBuilder.com. In March of 2005, *The Wall Street Journal* reported, "Rank and file employees are lying more often at work, by some measures." In its WorkUSA 2004/2005 survey of more than twelve thousand U.S. workers across all job levels and in all major industry sectors, Watson Wyatt, a global human resources consulting firm, reports that only 50 percent of employees "believe information they receive from management" and 51 percent have "trust and confidence" in senior management.

Lack of trust in the workplace and marketplace is not new.

Daniel Yankelovich describes three waves of mistrust in businesses over the last seventy-five years in his book *Profit with Honor*. The first two crises of confidence—the Great Depression of the 1930s and Vietnam, Watergate, and severe stagflation of the late 1960s through 1980—were marked by a weakening of confidence in the free-market economy and public disillusionment in big business. Yankelovich believes the third wave of mistrust started with the Enron scandal in 2001, and executives as well as corporations are held directly responsible for the scandals.

Over the last seventy-five years, manufacturing has transitioned from mass production to mass customization and global production. More recently, businesses embarked on concerted efforts to institutionalize quality, establish strong brands, leverage technology, and improve the environment. During that same time, we have seen the press glamorizing highly paid business leaders, corporate scandals costing workers billions of dollars in retirement accounts, and intense pressure for short-term profits altering corporate strategies. Workers, once used by companies as interchangeable parts of a production line, are now known as knowledge workers whose creativity makes them the most valuable asset of a company.

We believe that major corporations, especially U.S. businesses, are now entering another post-industrial period, with increasing globalization of production, distribution, research/development, operations, marketing, and sales accompanying an expansion of the service sector and even greater utilization of technology. At the center of this era, we find the networked knowledge worker heavily dependent on timely and candid exchanges of information and ideas to out-innovate and outperform the competition. High levels of workplace trust will equip these networked knowledge workers to think together, work together, and succeed together.

We assert, without reservation, that trust in the workplace provides a distinct and useable competitive advantage for companies of any size, but especially for large, geographically dispersed companies. Businesses where employees freely exchange information and ideas, speak their minds, and pass along customer feedback—positive and negative—prevail over businesses that do not. Businesses make choices about which idea to productize or which market to enter, and trust alone will not rescue a company who opts for an inferior product or is overtaken by a more aggressive and innovative rival. However, a company with high levels of trust across much of its workforce can expect its employees to consistently perform better than competitors with low levels of trust.

So what does trust do for a business? Why should business leaders make an investment in a culture of candor and openness? Trust enables people inside of a company to rely on one another. In fact, we define workplace trust as the ability of different people and parts of a company to rely consistently on one another. Trust is both a uniquely personal expression and an organization-wide trait. Trust—at the personal level and at the organization or corporate level—occurs because company leaders and front-line workers embrace the economic value of a candid and open exchange of information and ideas.

On the personal or employee level, this means the sales rep who just closed a huge deal can rely on manufacturing to fill the order and the shipping department to get the product to the customer as quickly as possible. On an employee level, this also means the project manager of a "virtual" team with key players scattered around the world can rely on members of the team to commit honestly to deadlines, ask the hard questions on their minds, openly offer ideas, and alert fellow team members when problems arise. Contrast this with many workplaces where team members often commit to a team leader's deadline or critical path without raising the real concerns swirling around their worried minds.

Three attributes will foster trust at the employee or individual worker level across companies. Employees need to be assertive, cohesive, and candid in their communications in order to build trust at the individual or work group level across companies of any size. By assertive, we refer to workers who are willing to seek information to do their job, understand the company, serve customers, and beat the competition. Assertive workers ask the nagging questions on their mind, engage coworkers on hard issues, and suggest new ideas and alternatives. Cohesive workers are connected to and committed to their team of coworkers and the company in general. They are interested in listening to and learning from others, and they willingly share information and ideas. Cohesive workers sustain the corporate culture with their efforts to collaborate and contribute to the larger "good" of the company and its customers. Candid workers place a premium on accurate and timely information flowing throughout their work environment. Their candor encompasses truthfulness in the substance of their work and in their interactions with coworkers and managers. Candor anchors the integrity of the statistics, findings, or recommendations of their workplace communications. Candor also fortifies their relationships with coworkers and managers, making it possible to acknowledge mistakes and delays without the usual excuses or white lies. Candid workers are willing to offer constructive criticism and pass along positive and negative customer feedback because they understand that quality of information directly affects the quality of decisions made within their company.

As trust grows, collaboration increases with employees reaching out to others or crossing organizational boundaries to serve customers. *The Wall Street Journal,* in its September 15, 2007, edition, stated, "Most companies continue to assume that innovation comes from that individual genius, or, at best, small, sequestered teams that vanish from sight and then return with big ideas. But the truth is most innovations are created through networks—groups of people working in concert. To lay the groundwork for innovation, organizations must make it easy for their employees to build networks—talk to their peers, share ideas and collaborate." In its study of the one thousand publicly held companies from around the world that spent the most on research and development in 2004, Booz Allen Hamilton, a global strategy and technology consulting firm, found no relationship between spending on research and development (R&D) and the primary measures of economic or corporate success, such as growth, enterprise profitability, and shareholder return. The consulting firm found that collaboration is key to innovation and productizing innovation at the companies spending lavishly on R&D.

With high levels of trust within a workforce, information, knowledge, and ideas flow briskly among workers, sounding alarms early on weakly performing products or changing customer needs. Customer complaints do not get buried but receive prompt attention and analysis by people and systems. Market intelligence detecting changing needs of critical customer segments surfaces quickly rather than being held onto by employees fearful of being perceived as disruptive or not team players.

High levels of trust do not mean a mistake-free environment or a workplace where deadlines are never missed. In a culture of candor and trust, when deadlines start slipping, team members speak up and warn others. It means that when a team leader puts forth an inaccurate estimate of costs or an unworkable plan, team members ask questions and suggest alternatives without fear of retribution. In a company where people trust one another, workers focus on solving the business problems facing them instead of protecting turf. In a company where people trust one another, people cannot build bridges fast enough in their search for knowledge to do their jobs.

We do not endorse one organizational structure over another—even as advancing computer technology removes time, location, and distance as business barriers. Business winners and losers emerge from matrixed, networked, hierarchical, and flat organizational structures. History, culture, founders, leaders, size, competitive environment, geographical dispersion, production mechanics, distribution logistics, cost structure, customer base, and technology shape organizational structure and underlying processes. Leaders organize their enterprises to secure business success, organizational agility, and personal engagement among employees. We search for and measure three building blocks that drive levels of candor and trust company-wide or at the organizational level of a business:

- Accessibility of information, ideas, and people
- Transparency of structures and processes
- Visibility of candor

While companies differ in how they construct the building blocks, we have not discovered a company experiencing high levels of trust without significant company-wide growth in the accessibility of information, ideas, and people; transparency of structures and processes; and visibility of candor.

The building block of accessibility calls for a work environment where people communicate easily with others throughout the company—in person, via the telephone, online, and through all other ways. The company makes information and knowledge easy to search for and use. Employees enthusiastically seek information to do their jobs well, understand the business, and serve customers but also understand that accessible communications channels mean that information must be checked for accuracy, as both formal and informal communications pathways contain biased material reflecting the perspective of the originator, factually incorrect material, and deceptive material. Workers consistently share information and ideas with one another within unimpeded formal and informal communications channels. They pursue information with less regard for organizational boundaries and more emphasis on solving problems. Increased accessibility of information allows employees to take responsibility for their information needs.

Accessible people are key to building trust across any kind of organization, especially large companies. Leaders not only communicate company positions, but also make themselves available to listen to employees, answer tough questions, and change course when the "wisdom of the workforce" provides new and better direction. Leaders cannot depend on a quarterly all-hands meeting or company video, but must make themselves available in person and by e-mail, telephone, Web sites, blogs, and other means to engage employees and build trust. We believe research will confirm that human interaction expedites the trust relationship, and leaders interested in building high levels of trust will make sure that officers and managers are personally reachable for a wide range of employees. (It's also a good way for officers and managers to find out what is going on in the company.)

The second building block of company-wide trust calls for transparency of structures and processes, especially deliberations for important decisions. Trust flourishes when workers are able to see how decision making unfolds. With more transparent processes and structures, employees are able to see where and how to get involved in addressing key issues. Employees figure out where to find information, people, ideas, knowledge, and resources when even complex organizational structures or systems contain understandable and useable pathways. Transparency not only facilitates employee involvement in decision-making processes, but also secures widespread acceptance when key decisions must be made within a closed circle of employees for competitive or legal reasons. Moreover, transparency demonstrates the integrity of decision making—that decisions were made based on rational reasoning and concrete criteria instead of position or power of decision-maker, limited information, faulty reasoning, or favoritism.

Transparency has gained currency among companies in the post-Enron era mostly for the reporting of financial results. The transparency of structures and processes required for building trust reflects an organizational penchant for opening up the company's pathways so that employees can freely navigate to information, ideas, and people essential to their work and their success.

The final building block of company-wide trust calls for the visibility of candor within the workplace. Company leaders and senior officers must lead by example with candor in their communications and openness in receiving and using input. In Towers Perrin's Global Workforce Study of nearly ninety thousand workers in eighteen countries released in the fall of 2007, only 44 percent of workers felt senior management "tries to be visible and accessible." Employees trust leaders who not only explain the company's business direction and competitive challenges, but who also admit missteps, explain the rationale and context for actions, and use the ideas and feedback of workers. Communications channels must be widely seen as expediting the flow of accurate information, not just the latest corporate pitch. The company's processes, especially its compensation system, must visibly reward—with money and promotions—contributions to a work environment where new ideas are explored, constructive criticism is encouraged, and customer feedback streams quickly. Front-line managers and supervisors remain the most visible and credible sources of information for workers and must be equipped, recognized, and rewarded for sustaining a work environment where coworkers can consistently rely on one another. Jack Welch, former CEO of General Electric, puts its well: "If you reward candor, you'll get it."

What's going on in companies around the world is a rapid destratification of access to information, knowledge, ideas, and people. The press often covers the more sensational side of technology in the workplace by reporting on an employee who puts a company video on YouTube and e-mails coworkers the URL instead of going through the corporate communications department. Thousands of workers—in a matter of seconds—can now view an executive's memo or a customer complaint. E-mails, blogs, and social networks capture the back and forth of online conversations, showing not just conclusions, but developing rationales, changes of opinions, and multiple perspectives. An employee can e-mail a question to a CEO or even debate a point with a company's leader on a company blog. Strategy documents, market reports, competitive analyses, and customer surveys that used to fill binders on bookshelves at companies around the world are now searchable online at even small- to medium-size companies.

The rapid advance of computer technology brings companies and their employees ever more powerful tools to communicate. One can just as easily discuss a new product idea via e-mail with a colleague in Tokyo as in Tulsa. Virtual teams of geographically dispersed employees are so commonplace today that most workers do not even think about the underlying technology. Announcements that used to take days to distribute throughout a company now take a matter of moments. Whether videoconferencing a meeting with employees at distant locations with your laptop or checking e-mail via your smart phone, the pace of workplace communications continues to rocket.

The soaring volume of information in the workplace—now available mainly online—threatens to overwhelm even the most diligent employees. In fact, hundreds of e-mails per day is a normal day at the office for many workers. To e-mail, add iChat, instant messaging, Web sites, blogs, intranets, online learning, voice mail, and the expanding capabilities of wireless phones. *The New Yorker* confirmed this information avalanche in its August 6, 2007, edition: "Nearly two million e-mails are dispatched every second, a hundred and seventy-one billion messages a day." Easy forwarding and copying of e-mails to large numbers of recipients and spam erode the effectiveness of e-mail within the workplace.

Today's technology also makes it easier to detect obfuscation, lying, misleading, and withholding of information in the workplace. Workers can easily use online means to compare past statements of a prevaricating CEO and see how the competition is actually faring. Informal communications, whether in blogs, e-mails, instant messaging, or social networks, take yesterday's water cooler conversations onto a much larger stage with many more participants. The line between internal and external communications continues to blur with easy forwarding of e-mail and editing of documents meant for limited circulation. Almost anything a CEO says to a small group of employees quickly reaches huge segments of a workforce due to the ease with which today's computer technology facilitates information sharing.

Technology profoundly affects two of the building blocks of workplace trust: the accessibility of information, ideas, and people and the transparency of structures and processes. Technology dramatically increases access to information, ideas, and people, opening up a company's supply of expertise and experience to workers. It increases organizational transparency, helping employees navigate corporate structures and processes. Workers are able to discover the head of a project team or the floor plan of a building needed for a meeting using widely available search tools. Technology helps employees see how key decision making occurs and how an organization's framework streamlines or impedes work. Technology opens the door for employees to seek information to do their jobs, understand the company, and serve customers.

The final building block of company-wide trust focuses on the visibility of candor and openness within the workplace. While technology can certainly help a company's leaders reach employees quicker, it also eliminates many face-to-face personal interactions. Companies rarely pay for dozens of employees to fly to a common location when videoconferencing and online collaboration tools cost much less. We continue to assess the levels of trust established when computer technology connects coworkers in disparate locations and replaces most actual face-to-face personal interaction. For example, we see that coworkers in Boston and Hong Kong who take advantage of e-mail, videoconferencing, the expanding capacities of cell phones, and the array of online collaboration tools can not only work well together, but also build bonds of trust. Senior leaders of large corporations cannot personally meet with thousands of employees spread around the world, yet through technology most employees can easily see and hear their CEO and often ask questions. However, we continue to observe on a consistent basis that face-to-face personal interactions play a major role in initiating working relationships, trust, and engagement across any size of company.

Most medium to large companies establish a lineup of formal communications ranging from internal Web sites and print publications to town hall meetings and company holiday parties. All too often companies stuff the formal communications vehicles with company praise heralding the latest success or glamorizing the CEO. All-hands meetings or town halls have become "produced events" that often succeed in leaving unasked the tough questions on the minds of employees. In spite of the dedication of many communications professionals within companies, too many CEOs see the company's formal communications channels as conduits for distributing "their" information. These company leaders wage their war of words on yesterday's battlefield. Employees enjoy practically instant access to the largest amount of information ever. Debates on pushing or pulling information through companies have been largely replaced with online search engines, agents, filters, and cookies helping workers sift through the growing clutter of online information.

Today's workers use both formal and informal communications channels in their efforts to learn more, educate others, or share information and ideas. Informal communications channels encompass lunchroom conversations, instant messaging, online chats, unsponsored company blogs, e-mail discussions, telephone conversations, and methods of exchanging information and ideas that we have yet to encounter. The dramatic expansion of computing power stimulates the proliferation of laptops, cell phones, BlackBerries, iPhones, smart phones, and other wireless gadgets that drive informal communications.

Companies must intersect informal communications channels with formal communications channels. Formal communications channels—run by the company—must reach for the highest levels of accuracy, timeliness, and usefulness of information. Employees depend on company publications and forums for major announcements about business direction and organizational changes and to validate information circulating through informal communications channels. A company must establish formal communications channels that employees not only feel safe in using but also expedite business processes. Executives and managers must get over feeling threatened by the multitude of informal communications ricocheting around businesses today and open up as many access points as possible for informal communications to stream into and become a part of formal communications processes.

One way that companies are taking advantage of informal channels of communication is through online messaging. We are now witnessing the rise of company blogs where a company leader engages employees in online discussions or debates. The online exchanges of members of a project team, for example, are often more revealing about progress and obstacles than meeting minutes or formal team reports. An employee will begin the discussion of a new idea or approach with one or two trusted coworkers. The idea will be kicked around and circulated to others who are trusted or who have a particular expertise or experience or who have access to resources to develop the idea. Blogs are also being used informally by workers to discuss work, social, political, and personal issues. Too, we see employees in many companies connecting with other employees through online social networking tools.

Corporate culture, the dynamic collection of values and behaviors that shape the workplace and how people in a company work with one another and communicate with one another, deeply influences levels of trust within a company's workforce.

Corporate cultures are not closed loops, but reflect social norms, competitive environments, supply chains, location, and internal and external factors. For example, extensive media glamorization of highly paid CEOs or coverage of corporate scandals influences how employees in many companies view and work with their top leaders. One company's culture can honor heroism in employees unselfishly working excruciatingly long hours to help the company make its quarterly numbers. Some corporate cultures idolize the lone genius creating the breakthrough, while others extol collaboration and teamwork.

We find corporate cultures where courtesy and consensus squeeze out debate on new ideas, weaknesses, and alternatives. We find cultures so centered on respect—often in Asian countries—that constructive criticism is mistaken for disloyalty. In the world of high-tech companies, we find a "work hard, play hard" mentality pervades many corporate cultures, often driving away older workers with families and extremely valuable hands-on business experience. We see mini-cultures within large, geographically dispersed companies. In these global companies, with employees in numerous countries, one often encounters a headquarters culture focused on company policies, processes, and strategies at odds with workers around the world focused on customers and competitors.

We urge companies to examine how their existing corporate culture can increase levels of trust within the workforce. Or do certain elements of the culture need to be reshaped to foster a more candid and open exchange of information and ideas among workers? For example, in the cultures where courtesy, consensus, and respect dominate the culture, company leaders can begin to shift the work environment by openly seeking and rewarding feedback and new ideas. Officers can admit missteps, what the company learned, and how a stronger, more competitive company emerges.

There is no one-size-fits-all prescription for reshaping corporate cultures to create cultures of candor. Rather, we strongly believe in sustaining and nurturing cultural qualities that make a company unique and drive employee loyalty and performance. We continue to observe specific behaviors driving a culture of candor and include the following list as a guide to companies seeking to foster a culture of candor.

- Share information as widely as legally and competitively possible.
- Define loyalty to include pointing out weaknesses and suggesting alternatives.
- Reward dissent, constructive criticism, and feedback.
- Penalize those who mislead, prevaricate, lie, or obfuscate.
- Listen especially well to employees close to customers.
- Celebrate workers' creativity by evaluating and using ideas on the basis of merit, not the position of the proponent.
- Distribute bad news quickly and admit missteps.
- Make decisions based on the quality of information, not its origin in a formal or informal communications channel.
- Explain rationale and context for key decisions to workers at all levels.
- Require all officers to be accessible personally to employees.

In a culture of candor, workers ask the nagging questions on their minds and engage coworkers and superiors on tough issues because the work environment supports exploring ideas and discovering better ways of working. Employees feel trusted to think, communicate, and work both inside the box and outside the box. In a company with high levels of trust, coworkers include constructive criticism and customer feedback in discussions to move the company forward, not to penalize others. High levels of trust within a company can only be attained with employees connected to and committed to a team of coworkers and the company's culture in general. Connected employees are more likely to listen to others, learn from others, support coworkers, and participate in the company's culture. Trust equips employees to be willing to extend their working relationships past their individual experience and expertise. As trust grows, collaboration increases with employees reaching out to others or crossing organizational boundaries to serve customers.

There are two primary ways that an organization devolves into a workplace with low levels of trust: the tipping point and the turning point. In the tipping point, we see companies where a steady erosion of trust emanates from multiple sources over an extended period of time. For example, the CEO begins to sugarcoat bad news, HR obscures the costs of benefits, managers withhold information, and employees stop passing along customer complaints until one day this combination snowballs into low levels of workplace trust. In the turning-point scenario, we see CEOs or other leaders making false or misleading statements or omitting key information during a critical moment for the company. All the built-up trust within the workplace evaporates as a CEO attempts to delude the workforce on an impending layoff, merger, or other significant event.

We generally see a tipping-point scenario as well in building high levels of trust within a company. Elements of accessible information, ideas, and people; transparent structures; and visible candor support workers sharing their expertise, experience, and ideas and trust grows throughout the organization. At a certain tipping point, when a large number of workers are participating in the open and candid exchange of information and ideas, trust takes hold across an organization.

In contrast, we have observed few instances when trust builds significantly across a workforce as a result of a turning point. The notable exceptions are when a popular founder returns to restore competitiveness and integrity to a company.

So what are the early warning signs for a company that low levels of trust are impeding the flow of information and ideas throughout the workforce and stifling innovation? In this book, we include several assessment tools that measure specific levels of trust among points of organizational contact. For example, we assess levels of trust going in both directions between a manager and his or her employees. In a separate assessment tool we measure how much managers trust their superiors. In another assessment tool we assess the trust levels of front-line employees with company leaders or senior management. We have identified eight exchange points where low levels of trust consistently impede the candid and accurate exchange of information and ideas among key work groups.

We test and validate the exchange point data with targeted focus groups, interviews, and evaluation of any recent surveys of the workforce or of large populations within the company. The validated data forms the basis of a credibility map for each company, visually identifying the areas of the company with communications channels clogged by low levels of trust as well as the areas with communications pathways anchored by high levels of trust. Each credibility map is unique, based on the organizational structure of the company. This visual representation takes trust from the "be more candid" or "listen more" admonitions to identifying organization-wide trends as well as specific exchange points where levels of trust need to be raised. In identifying areas with high levels of trust, the credibility map helps in discovering processes operating within the current corporate culture that may be replicable in building higher levels of trust throughout the company.

We often run into CEOs and top officers of a company who cannot imagine that workers in their company do not pass along constructive criticism and customers' complaints or ask the tough questions. We do not criticize these judgments but instead provide a more quantitative look at trust through the assessment tools and the credibility map. Many officers of large corporations are insulated from the give and take of information and ideas in the workplace. In hierarchical organizations, we find officers often insulated by layers of management filtering information into briefings, reports, and recommendations. In flat organizations, we often find officers overwhelmed by the sheer number of workers within a reporting relationship or two and unable to make meaningful contact with the various teams, individual contributors, and managers in their organization.

The assessment tools and credibility map clearly identify areas of weakness and strength for workplace trust. At the organizational level, we use these tools to assess the efficacy of each of the three building blocks of workplace trust. For example, with the assessment tools, we look at accessibility and discover organizations where workers are able to easily search for and use information to do their jobs but where company leaders and management in other business units are not available for even e-mail conversations. Transparent structures and processes, another building block of workplace trust, enable workers to reach across traditional organizational boundaries in solving problems. We find many large companies obscuring leverage points of human and physical resources by not providing clear pathways for workers. The final building block, visibility of candor, is disclosed in the assessment tools as workers and managers identify not only whom they trust but also how those bonds of trust were built. In other words, does a mid-level manager trust the CEO because they once worked together or because the CEO discusses the rationale for decisions, admits missteps quickly, and listens to and uses workers' suggestions?

We do not pretend that raising levels of trust across a large organization is easy. The process of rebuilding workplace trust requires a consistency of effort at many levels over an extended period of time. These efforts at rebuilding trust or just increasing levels of trust can be nullified or delayed by a few misstatements by company leaders on an impending merger, layoff, or reorganization.

Workplace trust may be the greatest untapped expeditor of business processes. It also may be the cheapest in terms of capital outlays, as increasing candor and openness in the workplace requires very little new equipment or buildings. The financial payoff awaits companies who abandon spin and stop misleading their workforces.

Chapter Three

Individual Trust and Candor in the Workplace

"You must trust and believe in people or life becomes impossible."
Anton Chekhov

In this chapter we aim to be candid about candor and trust in the workplace. We will investigate why employees at all levels often demonstrate a lack of candor, with negative consequences for workplace trust, relationships, morale, productivity, feedback, and innovation. On the flip side, we will see what companies can achieve by insisting upon trust and candor as core values of the organization, internally and externally. In Chapter 7, we will describe specific ways by which companies and individual employees can encourage trust relationships, measure them for analysis and planning, and reap their rewards.

Grasping the real meaning and value of workplace trust requires facing up to the difficulties of being candid at work and understanding why a lack of candor is so tempting at times. We may find that many moral and religious injunctions, including their calls for trust and candor, are blanket propositions that don't lie without wrinkles on the actual ups and downs of business experience. The problem with Sunday School is Monday morning. We seek a personal understanding of workplace trust in its complexity, bumps and all, not as a way of weaseling out of tight spots through dissembling and equivocation, but instead as a way of fairly estimating what's at stake and what to do when we have to choose options, perhaps involving degrees of trust.

Degrees of trust? Common sense tells us that at times a higher moral imperative may override any obligation we may have for being completely candid. We think twice before divulging information that may have a devastating impact on the lives of others, including our answers to queries from the boss such as, "Tell me whenever you see someone who isn't working hard on company time." We also have a natural tendency to protect ourselves. At a pinch point in our professional lives when absolute candor may endanger our careers in small or large ways, our minds understandably drift toward considerations of our mortgage or rent due every month, our financial responsibilities as partners and parents, and perhaps our slim chances of finding another job in a tight labor market. None of us opts easily and willingly for our own professional destruction. If we think that we are incapable or entirely inexperienced in bending, disguising, or avoiding some harsh realities about our work lives, that's the first lie we've told ourselves and probably not the last.

As we explain in the following chapters, we advise a posture of candor in professional life and, for that matter, personal life as well. The *Random House Webster's Unabridged Dictionary* defines "candor" as "the state or quality of being frank, open and sincere in speech or expression; freedom from bias; fairness." We prefer not to limit the concept of candor to a narrow definition, not because we want to waffle on the value of candid statements and behavior in business but because we want to tell its entire story: its complexities, its difficulties, and its ambiguities.

In its original Latin root, the word "candor" had no particular ties to veracity in itself. Instead, the word meant "to shine," as captured in related words such as "candle." That's the sense of honesty we want to convey and recommend in this book: professionals whose inner integrity and moral intentions "shine" to those around them, shining light on work relationships and business processes.

We also want to be clear about what this book is *not* about. It is not an exposé of unethical CEOs. Their antics already have been well chronicled in recent headlines. We are interested here in the hidden story of employee trust and candor at *all* levels. We contend that if millions of rank-and-file workers speak and act with a lack of candor, their distortion of business information and processes vastly outweighs the damaging influence of a few dishonest business leaders.

We do not present a rose-colored vision of business life as a theme park where the candor ticket always attracts friends and wins a prize. In fact, candor in business matters large and small can sometimes prove to be a lonely path with few cheerleaders along the way. Even your bosses may take you aside to urge, "Don't be so rigid. Let it slide." As the following chapters make clear, "sliding" has distinct consequences for you and for your company.

Mistakes versus Deception

At times, any of us can be genuinely wrong, with the result that others are deceived and often disappointed. In this case, we have made a mistake. We haven't intended to mislead. For example, we tell the boss that a customer order for eighty-five units of our product will be coming in before the close of the quarter. In fact, the customer orders only fifty-five units. Have we shown a lack of candor in order to make ourselves look good or have we simply made a mistake? The answer depends on factors that only we ourselves know: Did the customer say he would be ordering eighty-five units? Did we slip up and confuse one order with another? Did we make a math error? If we can answer yes to any of these alternatives, we know we have made a mistake without the intention of deceiving the boss. In other words, the litmus test for candor turns on whether we knew the actual situation and purposely spoke or acted in contradiction to what we knew.

Of course, the boss can rant, "You weren't being straight with me! I was counting on those eighty-five units you said the customer would order. I put myself on the line. What am I supposed to tell the vice president when my numbers come up short for the quarter?" These charges can be answered only by relying on a firm conviction of what we intended. When we make a claim that turns out to be false (in this case, the claim of an order for eighty-five units) and when that claim does us some temporary good (making us look good for the boss or increasing our bonus), others will often be quick to connect the apparent dots and accuse us of being less than candid. Especially at these moments when we "look bad," our own sense of integrity must be solid if we are to continue to hold our heads up as professionals. If we have made a career out of major and minor deceptions, we ourselves can eventually be confused as to whether we goofed or "pumped up" the actual situation. If we don't know what we actually intended, we cannot rebut the charges of others that we purposely deceived them.

Candor and the Business Habit of "B.S."

The situation is similar when it comes to "blowing smoke," a phrase that substitutes in polite company for plain old B.S. Let's say that we get on our soapbox during a break at a convention and tell people we have just met that "my company is a great place for women to work. There's no 'glass ceiling' that keeps women from rising to top management as easily as a man." We are speaking from our impressions and personal, limited knowledge of the company. As far as we know, we're being candid. But in fact we don't know how our company measures up when it comes to the hiring and promotion of women. Out of pride in where we work, we're certainly guilty of a degree of puffery or B.S. But have we purposely deceived others? No, if we spoke genuinely about our experience with the company. Yes, if we knew before speaking that the company had an average or poor record in promoting women—say, for example, that only two women out of fifty executives had risen to the rank of senior officers. The difference between B.S. and deception lies not so much in our intention (in this case, to make our company look impressive and attractive to our listeners) as in our knowledge of the actual situation.

That being said, it's true that "B.S.-ing" often comes perilously close to outright distortion and deception. Let's say that we know we don't have the full story or facts at hand before making a large claim to others. If we make it appear that we "know it all" even though we know in advance that we may be quite wrong about a situation, we've gone beyond garden-variety B.S. to some degree of purposeful deception. The degree of our deception then depends on what we intended. Are we manipulating others by our purposely exaggerated or incorrect claim?

The Actual Situation Is Not Always Obvious

Let's grant that the following equation is correct, at least for a base 10 numbering system: $2 + 2 = 4$. Are all or even most situations in our professional and personal experiences so fixed and obvious? Of course not. The accurate state of affairs for many business circumstances does not leap out as a clear, unambiguous statement or conviction.

Let's say that the boss asks you, "Are you happy working here?" We intend to be candid, but in our efforts to respond to the question, we confront difficulty in coming up with a simple answer. We mull over all the things that we dislike about the job (perhaps blunt questions from our boss!) and weigh them internally against the things that we like about the job. Dozens of experiences and impressions about our work life crowd into our judgment as we try to arrive at a conclusion that we can state in brief form with some conviction.

The boss notices that we seem to be stalling and prods,

"Come on, just give me your real feelings." Even that nudge hides very real complications. Our feelings? Like our memories and impressions of the workplace, our feelings about it cannot be instantly summed up. We often don't know exactly how we feel, yet to answer, "I don't know how I feel" isn't being candid either. We know we have feelings, but they are jumbled and inconclusive. In the British phrase, we "muddle through" our work without drawing firm or easily communicated conclusions about it. We don't have an internal calculator that sums up 12 negative impressions and balances them against 14 positive impressions to reach the conclusion that we are more happy than unhappy at work. Even our impressions themselves are fuzzy: Do I like working with my secretary? Yes and no. Do I like my retirement plan? Yes and no. Do I trust my boss? Yes and no.

The fuzziness of many work circumstances extends to most of the important things we talk about every day. To keep ourselves from purposeful deception or B.S.-ing, we often preface our statements with qualifiers such as "I think" or "I'm not sure, but . . ." Although these disclaimers technically put others on notice that our words should not be taken as gospel, others often draw firm conclusions from statements that we intended to be impressionistic and quite inconclusive. By so qualifying our statements, we are trying to be candid about the limits of our knowledge or conviction.

For example, at lunch a top company executive, Linda, says "*I think* the company is moving toward another round of layoffs." On the basis of her words, a colleague at the table dusts off his resume and a few days later finds a job with a competitor, a job he takes reluctantly to avoid being laid off. When his original employer does not lay off anyone, he confronts Linda: "You said there would be layoffs!" Linda recalls her exact words: "No, I said 'I think' there were going to be layoffs. I wasn't sure. Maybe I was being too cynical that day."

These comments come as somewhat empty explanations to the person who has acted as if these words were a statement of fact: "You should have made it clear that you didn't know what you were talking about. You're an executive vice president, Linda. We all assumed you had the inside track on what was going to happen in the company." Linda can't justify her words by saying, "But I was just giving my opinion. I gave you my candid impression." Her listeners have a right to reply, "That's the point—it's *your* opinion as a company leader, and that carries a lot of significance."

We don't entirely escape responsibility for the assumed meaning of our words. For this reason, stock brokerage firms accompany any specific investment recommendation with explicit language reminding investors that "past performance is no guarantee of future performance" and that "this investment involves the risk of financial loss." In our daily professional lives, the dividing line between being candid versus using imprecise, inconclusive communication lies in what we can reasonably assume about how others will understand our words. If we know in advance how others will take our words, candor requires that we put them on clear notice regarding the uncertainty of our reservations about our claims. We don't let them go down a blind alley if we know beforehand that they are likely to count too much on the certainty of what we say.

Candor That Impacts Others Negatively

Sometimes we delay, distort, or withhold candid responses because we do not want to damage others. As an extreme case, imagine Nazi soldiers during World War II busting down the door of a home and demanding, "Tell us if any Jews are hiding here!" Is it candid to respond, "Yes, Anne Frank is hiding just behind that wall"? It may be candid in a narrow sense, but entirely devoid of moral responsibility. To say, "I don't know" in this situation is literally false. You do know who is hiding in your house. These words invite investigation, saying in effect, "I don't know, so why don't you come in and find out?" The right thing to say from a moral perspective is clearly, "No one is hiding here." We face the irony that doing the right thing at a higher level of ethics may involve being less than candid at a lower level of ethics. In daily professional life, we don't face these kinds of epic moral and theological questions. But we do confront awkward moments when the welfare of other people will be impacted by what we say—or don't say.

Candor Has a Shelf Life

An additional complication in trying to be candid lies in the time sensitivity of what we say. When we make a claim, we do so on the evidence of the moment: "My employees are working hard to meet the deadline." Five minutes later the circumstances may change significantly (as we find out, for example, that some employees aren't working hard). Can we say, "I was wrong"? In fact, we weren't wrong, at least at the precise moment when we made our original claim. It would be accurate to say, "I've changed my mind." But how often should we qualify our conclusions to account for the passing of time and changing of factors? Every few minutes? Every few seconds?

The point here is that candor doesn't always sit conveniently still. We may make sincere statements based on our conclusions at one point in time only to look quite wrong shortly thereafter due to changes wrought by the passing of time. This is often the case in making statements about market conditions. Let's say that, in our view, customers may be ready for new capital expenditures, and we may say so in an important company meeting. The next day it becomes apparent that customers are actually pulling back on new spending. Were we being less than candid in the meeting? Of course not. We called the situation as we saw it at that time. We were right yesterday, though our words proved to be wrong a day later.

We usually don't keep an elaborate record of precisely what we knew and when for each of our statements. Inevitably, we sometimes appear to be less than candid with others when our statements prove to be in contradiction to the unexpected twists and turns of time and circumstances. In fact, the fault lies not with our intentions or intelligence but with the nature of circumstances themselves: they constantly change on a split-second basis.

Being Candid in a General Way

Our efforts to be candid at work get even murkier when we make interpretive statements based on limited evidence. "Investors were worried about the fall in new home sales," a television business analyst says on the nightly news, trying to explain a 100-point decline in the Dow Industrial Average. Did some investors somewhere worry about the fall in new home sales? Probably. But is it an expression of candor to say that all investors, or even a significant majority of investors, had such worries? The analyst doesn't know. He has created a general statement based on what he guesses, not what he knows for a fact.

Here's the difficulty with generalized candor: people accept it as fact and make it the basis of future action. In the case of housing sales, a listener might well conclude that the stock market will decline every time there is a fall in new housing sales. When the opposite occurs—the market rises in spite of a fall in new housing sales—the television listener loses trust in the TV analyst: "Wait a minute! You said that investors worry when new housing sales fall and that the stock market declines as a result. What gives?" If the TV analyst had the opportunity to rebut these charges, he might say, in all candor, "Look, I wasn't trying to deceive you. I thought maybe the stock market decline had something to do with the fall in new housing sales since they occurred on the same day. But I didn't say I had some kind of scientific survey of investors worldwide to back up what I said. I just made an educated guess."

Therein lies the problem with generalized candor. We don't warn listeners that we are generalizing based on slender evidence or no particular evidence at all. The TV business analyst doesn't preface his words by saying, "Candidly, I have no factual basis for what I am about to say. It is pure speculation." Instead, he presents himself on camera as a serious professional who seems to know why economic events are unfolding as they are. He speaks candidly in a general way but seldom, if ever, points out how flawed and unreliable his generalizations may be.

The Slippery Slope of Compromising Our Candor

In our personal and professional lives, we discard strategies that don't work and reuse strategies that get us ahead. These choices are based on pure pain-or-pleasure decision making. We avoid touching the hot stove twice and opt instead for what brings comfort, advantage, and good feeling. This natural tendency applies to our use and abuse of personal and professional candor.

Being less than candid often appears to get us out of a jam. We remember times we "dodged a bullet" by hedging on candor. Let's say we missed our deadline for completing an important report. "The copy machine was down," we say. A customer order has fallen through the cracks? "We've been having network problems," we tell the client. Such lack of candor has the immediate result of buying us time and helping us save face. But at what cost?

The problem with statements that compromise our candor lies ironically in the fact that they work so well. They get us off the hook in minor situations, and we begin to rely on them for rescuing us in increasingly more significant moments. A client reminds us that his order was promised for delivery by May 1 but is now late. We slip further down the slope of a lack of candor by telling our boss, "I told the client we would try for May 1, but I made no promises. That guy must have misunderstood me."

And the beat goes on. Fast-forward in our careers to the desperate moment when, as CEO of a failing company, we stand before TV cameras and claim, "I had no knowledge of the actions of company accountants. The statements I made to reassure stockholders had nothing to do with keeping our stock price up until I disposed of my personal holdings in the company." At this point, the learned habit of playing fast and loose with candor has spawned a monster, one that is all too familiar in recent business developments.

People Who Will Misuse Our Candor

Do we automatically owe candor to those we know will misuse it? In other words, are there people who don't deserve our candor? For example, your boss, a senior manager in the company, has made it clear that he despises what he calls "token hires" of minorities in the company. He has made it his personal mission to highlight the mistakes and misjudgments of anyone he has identified as a token hire. You have Richard, a new African-American employee, working for you. The boss stops you in the hallway: "I've got my eye on Richard. Let me know in detail how he's doing." Do you speak candidly and completely, telling the boss that Richard seems to be trying hard but still makes many mistakes requiring your close supervision, in the full knowledge that your boss will focus only on Richard's negatives and make much of these failings in an ongoing war with the company's affirmative-action program? Or do you gloss over Richard's work record, leaving your boss with the impression that he is doing reasonably well? Or do you stall for time, inventing some reason why you can't give your boss an answer at the moment: "Let me check my notes. I'll get back to you."

If you were to talk out the nature of this dilemma to yourself, it might take the following form: "My boss is a bigot eager to tear down the work of the few minority workers employed in this company. I don't want to feed him information that I know he will use destructively and unjustly against Richard. If I give my boss a list of Richard's recent mistakes, he will highlight these to give a biased impression of Richard, maybe even getting him fired. Yet if I don't give my boss the list, I will be disguising what I know about Richard's problems on the job. I want to be candid, but what's the right thing to do when it involves a deeply wrong person like my boss?"

These are the kinds of issues faced by anyone striving to build trust within the workplace. That path is not easy at times, nor does it always lie clearly marked before you. Nevertheless, our most important work relationships are based on our candor. In the face of ambiguity after ambiguity, we never stop trying to be a candid, trustworthy person.

Chapter Four

The Corrupting Influence of a Lack of Trust

"If you tell the truth, you don't have to remember anything."
Mark Twain

Most of us don't have to strain our imaginations to call to mind an organization where the "trust needle" is verging on low or empty. At some point in our careers, we have probably had the misfortune of spending time in such a company. One could hardly call it working, though it certainly felt like work in the negative sense. We observed the lack of trust in how workers related to one another, how managers treated employees, and above all in how employees regarded the company. Virtually all the building blocks of trust were damaged or missing.

Candor was in short supply. Coworkers, superiors, and subordinates said whatever they had to in order to avoid the wrath of the person above them in the pecking order. Often candor collapsed for the sake of personal convenience. It was simply easier to make up a story for the client than to complete the job. One story, of course, had a habit of necessitating several more. Lack of candor had a way of festering.

In this kind of environment, we came to work expecting that much of what we heard and read was going to be less than accurate. Lacking trust, we often wished that people would simply speak their minds spontaneously instead of having to plan out their answers, making sure that their previous stories were not being contradicted by the present one. "I'll get back to you on that" was a familiar refrain, no matter how straightforward the question.

Assertiveness was only a word in the dictionary. Sticking one's neck out to make an original comment or observation in a meeting was professional suicide, or so it felt. The old guard employees quickly taught the new hands (by example, if not words) that volunteering opinions, especially constructive criticism, was simply not done. Large or small, meetings presented the ridiculous prospect of otherwise bright people sitting stolid and stubborn, allowing the meeting leader to drone on aimlessly and purposelessly due to the lack of any discussion or input from others.

Cohesion was missing in action. Just as it seemed dangerous to speak up in meetings, so it appeared fruitless to band together with coworkers to get work done. Although we may have been assigned to a team, that collaboration was in name only. Typically in team meetings we got together only to divvy up assignments, then went back to our accustomed solitary style of work. Teams in this context turned out to be just a list of individuals. The whole was distinctly *not* greater than the sum of its parts.

A lack of trust in organizations has consequences. The following partial list of those consequences is not intended to be unsettling or depressing. Nevertheless, the symptoms of a trust gap must be faced squarely if we are serious about finding solutions.

Employee Morale

When one's work life feels like slow death, there is little motive to take pride in work, encourage coworkers, enjoy problem solving, celebrate achievement, or look forward to the camaraderie of interesting, engaging people. Everything shades toward gray. We are putting in "butt time" by placing our body in a paid environment for eight hours a day. But our spirit and sense of self—at least what remains of those precious qualities—is elsewhere entirely. We can become so enervated by such a dismal work environment that we no longer find the strength to think of how to escape. We're stuck, with only the calendar to rescue us at the end of our thirty-year sentence.

In this context, employee morale is not a "nice-to-have" for companies; it is one of the primary "must-haves" for productivity and the bottom line. Hopeless, unengaged employees who have given up caring about themselves and one another certainly have no energy or reason to care about the priorities of the company. They are (and act like) inmates. Managers become wardens and the company becomes a mini-welfare state, responsible to begrudgingly pay the very workers it despises. In such companies, leaders privately view layoffs and widespread terminations not as regrettable economic necessities but as payback. These leaders subscribe to the 80/20 rule: 80 percent of workers do virtually nothing while 20 percent carry the work load.

Employee Retention and Turnover

When members of an organization do not trust one another, they have one less reason to return to work each day. The paycheck may bind them to their job for a period, but as soon as that dollar amount can be equaled or exceeded by a more human and enjoyable work environment, they quit and move on. The fast-food industry had to learn this difficult lesson with its sixteen- to twenty-year-old workforce. The minimum-wage pay scale alone was insufficient to bring these young workers back to the job each day. Money spent in training them to do their jobs was largely wasted if, within a month or two, they were off to another employer, and often a competitor at that. Here's how one nineteen-year-old counter clerk at a nationwide fast-food franchise describes her situation:

It just wasn't fun at work. None of my friends worked there. It was incredibly boring to do the same things over and over, watching the clock to the second for breaktimes. There wasn't anything to talk about. We all felt like robots. After a month of that routine, I found another job in a small cafe. It was actually a little less money, but the lady that owned the shop talked to me about her business and kind of took me under her wing. She trusted me to use my brains and do the job right. A girlfriend of mine also worked there, so that made it a great situation.

It's easy to sneer at the work attitudes of nineteen-year-olds. But their core concerns reverberate throughout age groups and work categories. We all want a workplace where we can be ourselves with coworkers and bosses, where we trust others and are in turn trusted by them. When we lack that human connection, the mere dollars in the paycheck are insufficient to keep us coming back to work. As soon as we have a better option in terms of an environment of trust, we grab it. In this regard, business magazines such as *Fortune* and *Forbes* publish articles on "the 100 best places to work" rather than "the 100 top-paying places to work." The publishers realize that their readers are much more interested in the "total package" involved in the work environment than in the dollars alone. That package is described largely in terms of how bosses treat subordinates and how coworkers treat one another. In a word, employees are seeking a work environment characterized by mutual trust. When they find it, they stay. When they miss it, they leave—and expensively so, since the company must then rehire and retrain. Failure to retain employees thus becomes a significant blow to the bottom line.

Employee Recruitment

Attracting an employee a company wants has been described as a wooing process on both sides: the candidate tries to put his or her best foot forward while the company is also trying to show itself in the best light possible. The trust gap sours that budding relationship, as in this recruitment horror story told by a former senior HR officer.

> We knew we were offering salaries at or even slightly above those offered by our competitors. We couldn't figure out, therefore, why so many of our top candidates said "no thanks" to us and "yes!" to the guys across the street. When we did follow-up phone interviews, we never got anything conclusive. Former candidates would say vague things like it didn't feel like a good fit. Finally, one person who turned us down gave a straight answer to the question why. He said he talked casually with some of our workers during his plant tour. They told him it just wasn't a very good place to work. He got the impression we had an "us against them" workforce when it came to employee attitudes toward management. He got the impression that no one trusted anyone else in the company.
>
> When that message filtered through to top management, the solution was classic—and the primary reason why I myself quit the company. The CEO bristled at the idea that workers were talking to candidates. "From now on," he bellowed, "we're not taking candidates on plant tours. Don't let them talk to anyone!" In fact, the company rented an off-site office where it could conduct hiring interviews without any possibility that candidates could catch wind of the negative atmosphere in the company.

Companies can't recruit and hire antiseptically, even for their top candidates who have been solicited by headhunters and courted at the finest restaurants and hotels. At some point in the recruitment process, the company must put real people face-to-face with the candidate. That's when the presence or absence of trust in the company inevitably comes into play. At the end of a job interview, the candidate often asks the interviewer, "Have you enjoyed working here?" Hearing an enthusiastic yes can be the best persuader for a candidate trying to measure the human atmosphere in an organization as well as its financial picture. A high degree of trust among employees at all levels can't help but show to an outsider visiting the company and contemplating employment there. Recruitment in an environment of low trust is a perpetual uphill battle for a company in its attempts to hide what the workforce really thinks and feels.

Workplace Issues

As made abundantly clear by the proliferation of work-related lawsuits, American employees face legal challenges at every turn from members of protected groups (which now comprise about 60 percent of the population). In 2006, Fortune 500 companies paid out an average of $6.7 million for claims related to sexual harassment alone. The new kid on the block, in terms of litigation, is verbal abuse, when it rises to a level of severity so as to create a "hostile work environment." Employers are now being sued not only for ill-chosen language used by their managers toward subordinates, but even for verbal abuse that occurs between coworkers.

Why does one employer face suit after suit while another employer in the same industry, with the same employee profile, seems to go for years without legal entanglement and expense? The answer, we believe, comes down to an environment of trust. Take three examples:

An employee and her boss "get into it" verbally over a mistake in the wording of a contract processed by the employee. In the high-trust workplace, the tiff gets ironed out over a cup of coffee. Apologies are spoken on both sides, with the mutual resolution not to overreact next time a work problem surfaces. But in the low-trust workplace, the brouhaha is the opening battle in all-out war. The offended employee stomps off to her HR or union representative. The manager is eventually called on the carpet and a statement is taken that describes his tirade to the employee, including the foul language he used. The situation escalates when a lawyer sees an opportunity for legal action against the employer based on "hostile work environment" provisions in EEOC and Title VII guidelines. The company, in turn, hands the matter over to its counsel. The outcome? A large settlement in favor of the plaintiff (notably, plaintiffs win about 75 percent of harassment and discrimination suits in court), a fired manager, a bruised employee (now probably with employment for life with the company, if she chooses), and a traumatized, confused workforce ("Did you hear what happened to George? What did he say? Did she really get that much money? Can I?").

As another example, a junior manager feels that his ideas are being stifled by his immediate superior in the company. In the high-trust environment, he sits down with that manager and discusses his concerns face to face. He knows that his frankness will not be held against him at performance review time. He trusts that his own motives—to give his best for the company—are also those of his manager. He wants to understand his manager's point of view and to make his own perspective clear. They meet, they talk, they understand one another, and they forge a better working relationship.

But take this same scenario in the low-trust environment. The junior manager, distrusting the motives of his immediate supervisor, goes "over his head" to a company vice president. That executive hears the story of woe; she responds by calling in the supervisor to discuss the charges leveled by the junior manager. The supervisor is incensed: "I never . . . he should have . . . I would have . . . I always . . . he doesn't," and so forth. From this moment on, the supervisor's relationship with the junior manager will never be the same. They thoroughly distrust and even dislike one another. The executive in charge of both of them has a double problem on her hands. Work relations between the supervisor and the junior manager become a day-to-day drama of who is doing what to whom, with no holds barred in the workplace version of guerilla warfare.

In the final example, the home supply super chain has grown quickly, with more attention given to profit-making activities than to personnel (or so-called maintenance) policies. Three women in the company notice that in the last twenty-four months men have been more likely to get promotions than women. A total of thirty-eight men received some form of promotion versus only twenty women. Moreover, the women note that the management training manuals supplied by the company use the masculine pronoun exclusively when referring to managers and executives.

In the high-trust organization, the three women meet with company HR officers to share their observation and request that appropriate action be taken. The HR officers quickly understand the situation and immediately put into place corrective procedures guaranteeing that gender is not a biasing factor in company decisions regarding pay and promotion. The three women receive a commendation from the company president for calling this matter to the attention of HR. Their action becomes part of their record and reflects well on each of their own chances for promotion.

But replay the same scenario in the low-trust company. Here the three women automatically assume that the company has conspired to hold down its female employees. They bypass the company's HR officers entirely, judging them to be "part of the plot," and go directly to the press. Their story makes headlines in business news around the country, so much so that company stock drops several points in expectation of an ensuing class-action lawsuit. Lawyers are quick to pick up the case on a contingency basis, and the battle is joined. Female employees in the company are interviewed by attorneys and urged to join in the class action. The company scrambles to protect itself by making sudden and ill-planned promotions of women and rewriting all management training documents (surely inserting "he or she" when referring to managers). Years later the lawsuit is finally settled in court, to no one's particular satisfaction. The women receive a settlement that, after legal expenses and distribution to the hundreds of members of the class, amounts to only a few months' wages. They have lost the zest they once felt for the company and the job. Many quit. The company loses millions of dollars; it gains awkward and soured relationships with many of its female employees. Trust will never be the word used to describe management-employee relations in the company again.

Wasted Managerial and Executive Time

The squeaky wheel principle definitely applies to managers and executives across industries. By general consensus, two-thirds of their time is given to only one-third of their people. These are the "high maintenance" individuals who have issues they insist on discussing endlessly with their superiors, enter into e-mail dialogues with the boss that end up shedding more heat than light, and dominate or usurp the agenda at every meeting of their work unit. Their bosses are chary of firing them outright. The negative qualities that make them lousy employees unfortunately turn into powerful weapons when pre- or post-termination hearings take place, as they surely will. Firing an obnoxious but smart employee can embroil a manager in testimony, depositions, hearings, HR sessions, and other official proceedings for months or years. So managers tolerate the jerks in their midst and give them an ear—hour after hour at times.

What animates problem employees? They are angry about some imagined or real slight or injustice. Often they crave the attention that comes from their antics and attitudes: John has a secretary and I don't. Barbara's budget is larger than mine. My office is smaller than his. I don't get the respect I deserve around here. And so on, ad infinitum. How anger, even justified anger, is handled in an organization speaks volumes about the level of trust among its workers. In high-trust companies, people do get upset—trust is no inoculation against emotion—but widespread trust does make it possible for people to share their strong feelings without the damaging effects of endless harping, personal attacks, and productivity-defeating "moods."

Here's an executive's description of how she preserved her own managerial time while also dealing effectively with an employee's complaints:

> I would characterize my work unit as a family, but not in the Disneyland sense. We struggle like a real family and have our temporary misunderstandings and temper tantrums. But what makes us a family is our ability to hold on to the value of our relationships with one another no matter what the issue of the moment. Linda, one of the supervisors in my group, was upset that her repeated request for two more assistants wasn't getting any action. She had written me three extended e-mails over the course of a couple weeks, to which I responded that I would check into the matter. I meant to get back to her sooner, but a month passed before I had a chance to dig into the situation. By this time, she had asked my secretary to block out a couple hours so that we could resolve the matter one way or the other.
>
> When I saw that large swatch of time blacked out on my calendar, I came unglued. "Who was managing whom?" I asked myself. I wasn't mad at Linda for making the request for assistance, but it angered me that she was driving her agenda so hard and assuming that I had nothing better to do. I saw a train wreck coming: if we held the two-hour meeting, I might get upset and say no to her out of spite. She in turn would blow up and take out her feelings on the project she was supervising. Although it was difficult given the feelings involved on both sides, I decided to take the high road and assume that Linda's heart was in the right place. She was trying to get her job done. In short, I decided to trust her—and to show that trust. I met with her for lunch and apologized that I hadn't found time to act on her request for additional assistants. I could see the irritation melting

away from her face; she visibly relaxed and ended up apologizing in her own way for nagging me so often about the request. "I just felt sort of desperate, since this project involves so much data input," she said. I understood the situation and we figured out a good staffing solution on the spot. But more importantly, she and I found that we could get through the real stresses and crises of work life without wasting time with showdowns, verbal battles, and interminable e-mails. We learned we could trust each other.

For managers trying to budget their time effectively, the answer to the squeaky wheel does not lie in ignoring it. It will continue to squeak, and all the louder for apparent lack of attention. The solution lies in building a culture of trust wherein "wheels" know they don't have to "squeak" to have their concerns addressed fairly. Workers abuse managerial time when they feel the only way to get the boss to listen is to throw a tantrum. In a high-trust work environment, people have simply decided to grow up.

Breakdown in Planning/Scheduling

"So, can I count on that date?" That's the customer's question as he tries to determine how much to trust you. Put another way, the customer wants to make sure that your commitment is firm before making his own plans and schedules based on that commitment. In high-trust environments, projections and schedules are not always accurate. People misjudge work flow, don't foresee interruptions, and get blindsided by unexpected delays. But here's the key: in high-trust environments people speak up to the best of their knowledge, without the intention to manipulate or deceive. The following short scenario makes the case.

A hospital had just ordered a large supply of surgical instruments from a medical supply house. The Operating Room (OR) director told the sales rep in mid-May, "We absolutely have to have these new instruments by September 15 because the hospital is opening its new cardiac surgery and transplant center on October 1. Will the instruments be here by September 15?" Trust was high between the OR director and the medical supply house. They had done business many times before, always with satisfaction on both sides. The sales rep wanted to maintain and even increase that high-trust relationship. "Your order is coming from Japan," the rep said, "and we've never had an order take more than ninety days. That means your shipment should be in by mid-August, well before your deadline." "That's great," the director responded, "I'll count on it."

Nevertheless, the instruments did not arrive until late September. The hospital opened its cardiac surgery and transplant center on October 1 but was not able to begin inpatient or outpatient procedures until October 15 because of the state-mandated testing needed on the new instruments. But did the sales rep break trust with the director? That depends on a number of factors. If the sales rep knew that many orders ran more than ninety days for delivery but did not say so to the director for fear of losing a big sale, then the rep was indeed being disingenuous and untrustworthy. This would be no less the case if the rep had no firm idea of when the shipment would arrive but pretended to be sure, again for the sake of the sale.

Here's what actually transpired, resulting in a sustained trust relationship between the OR director and the medical supply house. The rep was correct in saying that no order to date from Japan had taken more than ninety days. Entirely out of the rep's control, however, a shipping strike occurred, delaying delivery until late September. As soon as the rep found out about the shipping strike in early August, he contacted the OR director to make the situation known. Although the director was upset by the circumstances, he wasn't angry at the medical supply house. From information supplied by the sales rep and his own investigation, the director knew that the instruments simply could not be delivered by anyone until the strike was over. Trust, in other words, can survive unexpected events. Trust cannot survive purposeful deception. In this example, a disreputable sales rep would have put off the director by saying, "We expect them in any day" or "The network is down so I can't check right now" or simply by not taking the director's phone calls.

Scheduling and planning become almost impossible within low-trust organizations. Even though you cannot count on an individual's assertions to always be right (as in the case of the surgical instruments), you must at least be able to count on the sincerity of those assertions. Mutual trust requires that each party tells what he or she knows, no more and no less. When unexpected disruptions occur, the task of the organization then becomes to plan in such a way as to minimize surprises. Imagine, by contrast, the extraordinary task of a company that has to somehow plan around its employees' fabrications and purposely omitted information. The vagaries of daily life are enough for any organization; lack of core confidence in its people's assertions is a deal breaker in any planning or scheduling effort

Redundant or Inadequate Resource Allocation

"Follow the money" goes the advice in tracing the working of any complex organization and its transactions. Like a hound after a rabbit, the money tends to flow toward claims, internal or external, that the company deems trustworthy. R&D, let's say, has made its case for $10 million in funding for a new product that is expected to dominate its lucrative market niche. Note the levels of trust involved in this substantial funding decision for the company. Even when empirical evidence is mounted to support the request, the company must still make many decisions based on trust. Is R&D right that the product can be developed for $10 million? What are the actual chances of market success for the new product? Are market conditions changing in ways detrimental to the success of the new product? At base, company leadership must determine to what extent it trusts the reliability of plans and projections made by its R&D division.

It is at this juncture that games are played with trust in many organizations. Knowing that the pie of company resources will not be divided equally, divisions within a company compete for as much as they can get based on their assertion of need and opportunity. After the year's budget has been distributed and spent, many organizations find to their chagrin that they were conned by their own people. Marketing, for example, inflated its budget request for Internet advertising, knowing full well that Internet ad rates were trending steeply downward. Manufacturing put in a budget number for raw materials on the basis of the previous year's acquisition, even though company warehouses were bulging with unused supplies. Even the motor pool got into the act, exaggerating the so-called poor condition of the existing car and truck fleet as an excuse to buy new vehicles.

"What's going on here?" a CEO might well ask. "Can't I even trust my own people to be straight about their budget needs? Is everyone a robber baron out to grab as much as possible, with no concern for what's best for the company?" The answer to all those questions is disheartening in many organizations. Even at the highest levels of corporate power, claims and assertions are too often thought of as negotiating gambits, with no candor or trust value attached. They are merely trial "balloons" floated in an effort to gauge what is possible in terms of resource acquisition, not what is right, best, or deserved.

When all division heads are playing this game of exaggeration and deception, company decision makers inevitably guess wrong much of the time and put the company's money on the wrong horse. Not wanting to be caught in their schemes, divisions go to absurd lengths to spend their budget each year, setting the stage for receiving at least the same amount and preferably more the following year. This game is so widely played in organizations large and small that company leaders may despair of even imagining things in a different frame: a work world where trust underlies budget requests and where a manager would find it unthinkable to be less than candid about his work unit's resource needs. As the saying goes, there may be honor among thieves, but for many corporate leaders the question is whether there is honor among division heads.

Simply as a "what if" exercise, imagine that a corporate leader sat down her division heads and gave them the trust speech: "I am trusting you to make accurate resource requests for the good of the entire company, not simply to make your own turf greener. Your future with this company depends directly on respecting and honoring that trust. I have to be able to trust what you say as your considered best judgment, not your trickery. I know that you have to rely on your own people, who give you numbers that add up to your total resource request. Pass on the message to them: This is a trust-based company. No game playing. Fool with that trust and you're out."

Resources in that kind of company would flow to where they are needed. Redundancies and underfunding would be significantly reduced. Trust, in short, would prove to be the key to improving the bottom line.

Absence of Sensing Systems

An organism—or organization—needs to know the good news and bad news in its environment. For survival, a fish has to sense the worm in the water, but it also needs to sense the hook. Unlike a physical organism, an organization does not have built-in senses that provide updates on good news and bad news. Certainly the company leader, locked as he or she often is in an ivory tower of self-accumulated "yes" assistants, has difficulty finding out some of the most basic and necessary information required for business success:

- What do customers really think of our products and services?

- What market conditions will influence our business positively or negatively?
- Who is working up to their capacity in the company and who is dogging it?
- What do my employees think and feel about my leadership style?
- What would our customers like us to produce? What services would they like us to offer?

Here are three ways in which companies get it wrong with their internal and external sensing systems. (A fish, by the way, would last about two minutes if it made the same mistakes in its environment.)

In the first scenario, a technical rep says: "Customers told me loud and clear what they didn't like about our software. It was pretty on the screen, but it loaded too slowly. My company wanted to sell them a hardware add-on to make the software load faster, but customers laughed at that idea. Why should they buy more hardware instead of just switching to the competitor's simpler, faster software? I had a tough time answering that question. But even though I heard this message over and over, there was no hope passing it along inside the company. They never ask tech reps what we're hearing. There's literally no channel I could use—no meetings, no hotline, not even a company blog. And I'm not going to be the first to volunteer a bunch of customer feedback by e-mail to my bosses."

"I see customers every day," a sales manager explains in another scenario. "I haven't had a lunch without a customer in over two months. So I feel like I know a lot, pro and con, about customer attitudes and opinions. But here's the problem. Our company culture kills the messenger, if you know what I mean. If I shared some of the customer complaints I hear, I would be goring somebody's ox in the company. For example, if I told the VP of Marketing that customers gagged at his new ad campaign, he would take it personally and probably figure out a way to pay me back in some financially painful way. That campaign was his 'baby' and pity the guy in the company who has anything bad to say about it, especially after the CEO authorized a huge budget to pay for it. Basically, our company has shut off any channel through which bad news could be heard."

In the final example, we hear from a customer service rep: "I spend eight hours a day, five days a week, on the phone with customers who are having trouble with our products. Wouldn't it seem like a sane thing to do to have me keep a journal or a log of some kind so that these problems can be corrected? Believe it or not, we have nothing like that in Customer Service. We're told just to help the customer solve the problem, not to worry about any internal changes in the company. One boss actually told me, 'Brighter minds upstairs will take care of that.' Well, they may be brighter minds, but they sure aren't hearing what customers are saying. It's amazing to me that a big company doesn't want to collect intelligence on complaints from its customers."

In the first of these cases, the company locked out negative news in a structural way. The tech rep had no channel through which to convey what he learned from customers. In the second case, the company shut down negative feedback by its cultural norms. Anyone spreading such bad news would be viewed as a traitor of sorts, attacking programs that others had worked hard on and took pride in. In the final case, the company avoided bad news by deprecating the source—"she's just a customer service rep doing phone work" and "brighter minds upstairs will deal with any changes."

No matter how a company shuts down its sensing systems, the root cause comes down to a lack of trust. The company does not trust that its own people have the interest of the company at heart when they attempt to report back on negative customer feedback or other bad news. Those who have created programs and policies in the company don't trust the motives of any internal critic, even those simply reporting on what customers say. "It's a personal attack," they complain, "and a breach of loyalty."

Companies that restore trust as the top-to-bottom fabric of the organization reactivate their sensing systems. Because employees at different levels realize that other workers are not out to get them or their programs, they willingly listen to feedback and make adjustments accordingly. The fish example again serves well: scenting the good news of a meal-sized morsel in the water ahead is indeed important, but so is the ability to sense the subtle shadow from behind (the bad news) of a shark closing in for the kill.

Corrupted Decision-Making Processes

Any decision in business can be viewed as the roof on a house. It never stands alone, nor does it come first in the building process. Its size, composition, shape, and design depend almost entirely on the foundation and walls that support it. Similarly, a decision must rest upon stable, underpinning evidence and argument to have any validity or usefulness.

That's where trust comes in. How can worthwhile decisions be made at the top in an organization when the data, arguments, and recommendations underlying those decisions are untrustworthy? More than one municipality has been in this dilemma with regard to public funding of a sports stadium, bridge, or other mammoth project. Special interests, including real-estate promoters, retail business owners, and hospitality vendors, work with other lobbyists to hook the city or state into a huge project from which there is no turning back. Evidence is selected, gathered, and massaged, often by the municipal agencies themselves, to support what a mayor, governor, or legislation wants to see happen. Only when the decision has been made, sometimes literally as the ink dries, do the rest of the facts about the project come to light. Taxpayers often end up paying twice as much as projected due to faulty decision making by their leaders.

This problem is not unique to civic undertakings. Even a small businessperson can make the mistake of putting a roof on bad walls, so to speak. Consider the shop owner who stocks up on a particular inventory item based on the salesperson's word (unverified) that they are "selling like hotcakes" in a nearby town or the new accountant's mistake of borrowing heavily to install a version of sophisticated accounting software shown to him at a trade show. Dazzled by the persuasiveness of the salesperson at the show, the accountant fails to consider his clientele, made up largely of mom-and-pop customers who do not need and certainly do not want the "turbo" version of software he has just purchased.

This is all to say that decision making is not worthy of the name when it cannot trust—that is, rely on the candor—of its underlying assumptions. Companies with low trust levels can expect deeply flawed decision making not just at the top, but in the simplest matters of business life: buying three times the amount of copy paper required because an ambitious salesperson whispers that paper prices are going to double (they don't); deciding to send every manager to an off-site seminar touted as a huge productivity booster (it isn't); or asking every employee to contribute to the boss's favorite charity as a sign of loyalty (they won't).

Failure to Innovate

Doing something different inevitably involves a degree of risk that, in turn, requires courage. In a high-trust business environment, employees are willing to try new things as small as a new office procedure or as large as a new product line because they believe "we're in this together," that is, we are a team that does not condemn its individual members for innovative thoughts and actions. In this kind of environment, innovation of any kind becomes part of the fun and excitement of business life. Employees don't park their brains at the curb when they come to work, but instead arrive fully expecting to solve problems and create opportunities based on their unique abilities, not just the traditional approaches.

By contrast, consider the company with low trust. "What's the upside," employees wonder, "of sticking my neck out to suggest a new way of doing things? The people invested in doing things the old way will undoubtedly squawk because their routine and power base is being challenged. I don't trust them for a minute not to connive against me for even mentioning that there may be a better way or a better product."

Other employees, fully capable of innovating, hold back their creativity because "in this company, all good ideas have to flow from the boss." Innovation threatens many managers as a challenge to their authority and status. "How am I going to look," an insecure manager complains, "if some guy in another division comes up with an idea to revolutionize my products? I'll look stupid, as if I don't know my own business." That kind of thinking—revealing a deep mistrust of what others will think in the company—inhibits a great deal of potential innovation.

Sometimes the trust that's lacking with regard to innovation is a basic trust in one's own intuitions. In popular fiction and television, if not entirely in life, inventors are depicted as oddballs, loners, social recluses hidden away for endless hours in shabby labs and workshops. Whatever the actual facts involved in this depiction, the image makes the point that inventors have to have the strength of their own convictions. They have to follow their curiosity to where it leads, not to where it pleases the organization. This kind of stubborn trust in oneself is forward-looking in the sense that it seeks what can be, not what was. Inventors even put aside customer preferences at times, judging that feedback to be a measurement of past levels of satisfaction. As Henry Ford said, "If I had asked my customers what they wanted, they would have said a faster horse."

Contentious, Litigious Performance Evaluation

By and large, managers dislike preparing and delivering performance evaluations. Therefore, they do it as seldom as possible. Across industries, performance evaluations still tend to occur on an annual basis in spite of all research evidence suggesting that conducting more frequent performance evaluations has a beneficial effect on employee motivation, loyalty, and productivity. Here are three managers discussing their different dilemmas when it comes to performance evaluation time in the company.

"I put it off as long as possible, and then end up giving higher marks than I probably should just to keep from getting in a shouting match with my employees. After all, I have to work with them everyday. It's like grade inflation in school. Better just to give everyone a B+ and tell them they're doing fine, nothing to worry about. I don't trust them not to cause big problems for me if I do otherwise. Giving someone low marks means I have to be able to give chapter and verse examples of those behaviors when the offended employee drags me down to HR for a conference. One manager actually got a letter from an attorney threatening legal action unless she changed a negative performance evaluation she had given a person with disabilities. Who needs that kind of hassle? I don't get paid enough to fight with my employees."

Another complains, "I hate performance evaluations because they're not at all confidential, thanks to my big-mouth employees. They treat these evaluations as a horse race and won't rest until they find out what marks and comments each person got in the department. For the month following performance evaluations, I spend endless office hours meeting with employees who want to know why they got a lower score or less positive comment than someone else. Of course that puts me in a difficult position since I can't legally discuss anyone else's performance record with another employee. So, in self-defense, I end up giving everyone about the same marks. It's kind of a dead heat at the finish line, so to speak. Let them argue about that, if they can."

A third mamger describes another problem: "My company's system of performance evaluations doesn't work because there's not much trust between different levels of management. For example, I can't trust my boss to stand behind me on most of my performance evaluations. If I give one of my people negative marks, he or she will run, not walk, to my boss's office to tearfully complain about my biases, poor record keeping, negative attitude, or whatever. My boss has the 'listen to everything' approach to management, so he hears these people out. Usually he ends the conversation by saying that he will speak to me to get my side of the story. So I end up in a kind of court, with my boss as the judge and my employee as the plaintiff. A lot of the evaluation process comes down to a judgment call—mine, in fact, since I've observed these people for an entire year. But my boss often asks me to reconsider my evaluations and bump marks up just to keep some of his favorite employees happy—or to keep them from going to his boss."

Performance evaluations in low-trust organizations are a tragic farce, a play enacted with comic overtones and no happy result. Employees don't trust their manager to be just in his or her evaluation of their work. Managers don't trust employees to receive constructive criticism and use it to improve their work. The whole process is a wound that opens once a year. Left to their own preferences, managers in low-trust companies would probably not conduct performance evaluations at all.

By contrast, high-trust companies view frequent performance evaluations as opportunities for dialogue and feedback. We like to know how we're doing. Employees regularly complain, in fact, when they receive no feedback on the quality of their work. A high-trust work environment allows a manager to sit down with an employee to discuss openly and frankly the high points and low points of the work period under consideration.

The manager trusts that the employee does not come in to the evaluation interview with a chip on his or her shoulder. Conversely, the employee trusts that the manager brings no personal prejudice or animosity to the task of evaluation. Both are interested in a fair reading of the work record and an opportunity to set goals for the future.

Managers in this kind of environment also trust their bosses not to play court of appeals to their judgments. If employees know that they have a second bite at the apple by going above a manager's head, the initial performance evaluation loses most of its meaning. In exceptional cases, of course, upper levels of management should be involved, as in cases of obvious personality conflict, harassment, or other interpersonal problems between manager and employee. But these cases should be few in a high-trust environment.

Mixed Messages to Customers

In low-trust companies, each man is an island, reversing John Donne's famous quote. A customer makes contact with, let's say, a cell phone company only to discover that the New Accounts representatives have nothing to do with the Customer Service reps and that assurances made by New Accounts at the time of purchasing the cell phone service are treated like an uninterpretable message from the Dead Sea scrolls by Customer Service. It does no good for the customer to complain, "But they told me in New Accounts that . . ." The Customer Service rep interrupts to correct, "We're not New Accounts. Do you want me to transfer you to New Accounts?" Of course, the customer doesn't, because the matter at hand is something only Customer Service can deal with. New Accounts said so not five minutes ago. This madness goes on until the customer considers canceling his cell phone service altogether, only to discover that, by contract, he can't for the next two years. Then comes the cloying question from Customer Service, "Is there anything else I can help you with today?"

When the left hand doesn't know (or care) what the right hand is doing in a company, the customer suffers first—but the company suffers eventually. Far from trusting one another to serve the customer's best interests, New Accounts and Customer Service in the example above are virtual strangers, probably based in different states or even on different continents. New Accounts would be perturbed by Customer Service's statements to customers if New Accounts cared. But of course they don't. They have closed the sale. That is the end of their customer relationship. In turn, Customer Service could be annoyed at what New Accounts falsely told the customer about phone service at the time of the sale. But Customer Service doesn't care. It has no link to New Accounts and no desire to help them improve their customer relationship.

In a high-trust company, all units want to maintain and enhance the good name and good faith of all other units in the enterprise. A customer cannot be expected to trust one part of the company but not another. Revising the cell phone scenario above, a high-trust company would make sure that Customer Service and New Accounts spoke the same language, made the same claims, and stood behind the same assurances to customers. There would be no absurdities such as Customer Service saying, "I'm not able to transfer you to New Accounts, but I can give you their phone number." A phone company says this, mind you! Nor would New Accounts blather, "I can't give you my extension and I can't call you back at your number. You'll have to dial the 800 number again and wait in queue for the next representative." These mindless, excruciating conversations send customers over the edge into total mistrust of the company's motives and basic ethics. "I feel duped," a million cell phone customers must almost say in unison. "Everything was rosy when I signed the contract and they charged my credit card. But everything has gone downhill since then. Now I don't trust them at all."

Leadership Breakdowns

According to *The Leadership Challenge,* the well-known book by leadership gurus James Kouzes and Barry Posner, a true leader practices five behaviors:
- Model the way
- Inspire a shared vision
- Challenge the process
- Enable others to act
- Encourage the heart

In low-trust business environments, these behaviors either never get off the launching pad or backfire badly for the leader. When employees do not trust their leader, virtually anything he does can and will be interpreted to the leader's disadvantage. If a leader attempts to model the way by walking the floors of the office, the low-trust workforce will judge that she's spying on them. A company leader may try to inspire a shared vision by taking all division and department heads to an off-site retreat in the Colorado Rockies. "Just a junket," the low-trust workforce may cynically respond. "A chance for them to figure new ways to screw us." The same leader may urge workers to challenge the process, only to stimulate grapevine grumbling along the lines: "Fine for him to say, but you know what will happen to anyone who really tries to challenge anything around here!" The leader's efforts to enable others to act is misinterpreted as dereliction of his own duties and a penchant for convenient delegation. Finally, a leader's attempts to encourage the heart in speeches and written messages is dismissed as just another "rah-rah speech."

Leaders have obvious difficulty swimming against the strong tide of such cynical, low-trust attitudes on the part of the workforce. The behavior of a leader, even following the best practices outlined by Kouzes and Posner, may be doomed to failure unless trust relationships are present and healthy in the organization. The leader alone cannot hoist the trust level of organization up by its own bootstraps. In the case of many companies, the question of what's wrong with the CEO can well be answered by a companion question: what's wrong with their workforce?

In high-trust companies, the behaviors of leaders bear fruit for at least five reasons:
- Employees are eager to admire their leader and follow his or her example.
- Employees want a vision of their work life that dignifies their effort and supports their personal and social goals.
- Employees trust that challenges to the process will be viewed in the company as positive contributions to improvement, not as attacks or rebellions.
- Employees accept new responsibilities as signs of confidence in them on the part of their managers, not as punishment for perceived inactivity or laziness.
- Employees recognize that their hearts are involved in their work as well as their heads; they care about what they do and those they work with. Therefore, a leader's efforts to encourage the heart is welcome as a motivating and morale-building force.

Worker Cliques and Factions

The so-called grapevine has been studied for more than fifty years in organizations. Among the more striking findings of researchers are the following points.
- The grapevine will exist in an organization no matter what official sources of authority and community do or say. People will find ways to talk privately with others in the organization, if not on company time, then on breaks, lunch hours, and after-hours get-togethers.
- The grapevine will automatically exclude almost all authority figures, irrespective of their personality and sociability. The boss cannot choose whether to tune in to what the grapevine is saying. If someone within the

grapevine becomes a spy for the boss, the grapevine will tend to isolate and exclude that person.
- The grapevine does not treat all members equally. Those involved in the grapevine exercise judgment regarding who can be trusted with "hot" information, who is likely to have access to such information, and who may be prone to exaggerating or distorting information. Individuals who act as Grand Central Stations for information flow on the grapevine—those who seem to hear everything and tell everything—are liaison individuals. Those who hear news but have no one to pass it to (or choose not to pass it) are isolates—the dead-enders of the grapevine chain.
- The grapevine is highly credible for its members. They will tend to believe what's on the grapevine more than what is set down in black-and-white company documents and in executive speeches.
- The grapevine is lightning fast, especially when news breaks that affects many of its members.
- The fastest way to lose membership in the grapevine is to break trust with other members. Examples of such trust breaking include revealing grapevine information to nonmembers, refusing to share information with grapevine members who have shared with you, twisting grapevine information in a way that reflects poorly on the person you received the information from, and slowing the flow of grapevine information by not passing along information expeditiously.

In a high-trust organization, workers are far less likely to create or rely upon a "rumor mill" for information about their status as employees or company developments. Communications from company leaders, managers, and supervisors tend to be trusted in these companies because workers have no reason to doubt what their leaders tell them. By contrast, in low-trust companies, the grapevine quickly fills the vacuum left by a lack of credible information from management. As with any communication system that relies upon messages passed from individual to individual, often in secret, the grapevine usually exerts an exaggerating effect on the items of information it carries. What one boss said in supposed confidence about one underperforming worker gets blown out of proportion to represent what managers think about all workers. Morale suffers in such low-trust environments as participants in the grapevine begin to doubt their security in the organization and the motives of their managers.

Loss of Reputation in the Industry

Given the portability of careers in many business sectors in our day, it comes as no surprise that employees talk across company boundaries. On chat lines and blogs as well as at conferences, conventions, and the local bar or coffee house, employees compare notes on what it is like to work at company XYZ. Gripes and complaints, of course, have more entertainment value and often greater circulation than testimonials about why an employee may like his job. Companies with low trust levels, for the reasons explained so far in this chapter, open the door to a cornucopia of negativity.

The primary effect of a bad reputation based on a lack of trust among workers is difficulty in attracting talent. À la David Letterman, experienced employees can often tick of their personal list of the ten worst companies to work for in their industry. Reasons for inclusion on this list range from lack of respect for employees to harsh management style to poor benefits and promotion possibilities. Would-be employees take these criticisms seriously and often steer clear of problem companies they have been warned about by their peers.

Loss of Employee Loyalty

In many industries, the future belongs not to companies that can do more but to companies that know more, as evidenced by the immense market capitalization of Google stock. The easiest thing for an employee to steal while working for a company or upon quitting is valuable product, technical, or market knowledge. An experienced employee who crosses the street to work for a competitor is a virtual file cabinet of client contacts, market strategies, and technical tips. No non-compete contract to date has been successful in sealing the lips of an employee who is angry at his or her former employer and eager to impress a new one. Low-trust business environments encourage leakage of proprietary knowledge. In a perverse way, it feels good for a disgruntled former employee to share business secrets outside the company. The loss of trust that may have led to resignation or termination also underwrites, however wrongly, the temptation to disclose protected information to competitors.

High-trust environments do not prevent resignation and termination, although employees in a work environment with high levels of trust are less likely to quit. But trust does raise the bar on individual and corporate ethics. An employee who has been treated as a trusted partner is less likely to abandon his moral code to sabotage a previous employer by inappropriate disclosure of information. If low trust makes disloyalty feel good, high trust makes disloyalty feel bad—and therefore discourages it.

Abuse of Benefits Provisions

"I'm going to take this company for all it's worth as long as I'm here—every possible sick day, every personal leave day, even every pencil, pen, and ream of paper I can stick in my briefcase. They owe me for what they've put me through." Those are the words of a deeply discontented worker who now views the company's supplies and benefits as his means for vengeance. If the company and its managers don't trust him, he will sink to their expectations. In low-trust business environments, company property ranging from printers to laptop computers to calculators and desk lamps disappears due to employee theft. Low-trust companies end up posting inspection guards and metal detectors at company entrances, further enforcing the message to employees that they are not trusted.

This is not to say that high-trust companies never have employees who steal an occasional sick day to watch the World Series or take home a box of pencils for the kids. These infractions of company rules, however, are not conceived of and carried out as payback to the company or its managers for a lack of trust or other felt injustice. It's just human frailty in high-trust companies, and it happens much less often, probably because it doesn't need to satisfy any craving for revenge.

Careers with No Portability

Finally, the legacy of low-trust companies stains the resume of employees trying to move beyond the low-trust organization in their careers. It's easy to imagine the chilling effect on new employers of the word "Enron" or "WorldCom" on a candidate's application form. New employers are rightly concerned that bringing aboard an employee from a low-trust company with a bad reputation will prove to be a contagion of sorts. The employee's habits of low-trust interaction may exert a corrupting effect on at least a corner of a high-trust culture. If only for personal advantage, rising managers should avoid low-trust business environments if they care about the upward portability of their careers.

A lack of trust damages both individuals and their companies. But there's light at the end of that dark tunnel. We take on preserving employee trust, or rebuilding trust bonds that have eroded, in the following chapters.

Chapter Five

Common Trust Busters at Work

"Trust is the emotional glue that binds followers and leader together. . . . It cannot be mandated or purchased; it must be earned. Trust is the basic ingredient of all organizations, the lubrication that maintains the organization."

Warren Bennis and Burt Nanus,
Leaders: The Strategies for Taking Charge

It's one thing to say that employees at all levels within a company often fail the candor and trust test, resulting in a breakdown of trust bonds with peers, subordinates, and supervisors. It is quite another to understand *why* these otherwise upstanding citizens speak and act in such perverse, counterproductive ways in the workplace. Put simply, as we have put it in many employee interviews, why not be candid?

One of the most frequent answers to that question can be summed up as, "The devil made me do it"; in other words, "I was forced or manipulated into saying and doing things that aren't really 'me'." What are these mysterious forces that turn otherwise ethical individuals into people who don't speak up when they should or make statements that are less than candid?

The Angry Boss Made Me Do It

American business magazines lionize "the ten toughest bosses" and their temperamental antics. These behaviors in the European

Workplace Trust Busters

Promoting a yes-man or yes-woman whose career who has been largely distinguished by unquestioning loyalty to a person in power.

Grapevines, rumor mills, and informal networks beating formal communications channels on major announcements.

CEO or other top executive caught lying, cheating, stealing, or defrauding.

Employees reading first about company layoffs or merger in their local newspaper.

Managers instructing their work groups not to cooperate with other work groups or individuals.

Passing over for promotion employees who ask tough questions about company direction.

Constructive criticism ignored and career of employee offering such feedback derailed.

Company blogs where participating executives do not write their own entries.

Official company publications focusing more on bowling teams and beach cleanups than new markets or competitive threats.

Top executives receiving bonuses, large salary increases, and stock options while telling workforce that salaries and budgets across the company must remain flat.

Union are termed "bullying" and are grounds for termination as well as civil prosecution, but in the United States, some still cling stubbornly to the outmoded notion that a boss must be a "butt-kicker," rousing fear in the hearts of subordinates. Such actions, the theory goes, make employees toe the line and give their utmost effort, fearing punishment in various forms from the tyrannical boss.

Fear can be a powerful motivator, at least in the short term. Among the less desirable behaviors it motivates are widespread tendencies for subordinates to make up excuses, fabricate information, blame others to avoid personal responsibility, and play it safe by not speaking up at all. As one manager in Cincinnati explains,

> The CEO is well known for his temper, and all his lieutenants in the company have started using the same angry management style. They swear a blue streak in meetings if someone slips a deadline, even for legitimate reasons, or makes a mistake of some kind. We all feel that the office is a minefield where one misstep can get you maimed, if not destroyed professionally. So we tiptoe around out of fear of saying or doing the wrong thing. No one sticks his or her neck out, especially in meetings attended by the upper-level bosses. Candor? In this office? You've got to be kidding.

Another employee, this time at an entry-level position, continues the same story:

> Do I say what I have to sometimes to cover my you-know-what? Absolutely. So does everyone else at my level in the company. If something goes wrong—a crate gets dropped, let's say, with a lot of merchandise damaged—our first impulse is not to figure out what went wrong and how to correct it. Instead, we all scurry for cover by making up excuses to show that it wasn't my fault. It's like the game musical chairs as we all run for safety, and God help the poor employee who gets stuck with the blame. The boss

goes nuts, berating the person in front of the rest of us and putting him or her on the worst possible jobs for weeks or months. When the boss is so vindictive, what do you expect the employees to do? We sure aren't going to step forward to tell it like it is. The boss makes that impossible.

Mean bosses who manage by terror exert a corrupting influence on the willingness of their workers to be candid. These bosses destroy any chance that employees will trust them. Like children afraid of an angry father, the "kids" (i.e., workers) will do and say anything in the parent/boss's presence to avoid punishment, even if that involves giving up candor altogether. Bosses who rely on their tempers to motivate others have the illusion that they are achieving command and control over the troops. In fact, they are losing control and sacrificing trust in at least three ways.

First, these bosses don't know what's really happening in their organizations. The shock and awe of temper displays on the part of the boss make employees unwilling to reveal client feedback and information about company problems. These employees have seen the boss "kill the messenger" so often that they are rightly fearful of stepping forward with any information that might anger him or her.

Second, they don't have the loyalty of people who fear and despise them. Workers who have been cowed by savage outbursts of the boss's temper are not likely to be the ones who give their best to the job, stay late to finish an important project, or go beyond the call of their job description to contribute innovative ideas. The boss's angry outbursts send these employees fleeing to the exact language of their job descriptions—"I'll do exactly what my contract says and nothing more"—or to grievance procedures secured by a union. These emotionally and professionally bruised employees are probably the ones circulating their resumes to the competition in hopes of finding a less stressful, less punishing work environment.

Consider evidence from exit data interviews with employees who quit. The predominant reason employees leave a company has nothing to do with salary. Instead, the most frequently cited reason is that they did not get along with the boss. Such turnover proves exceedingly expensive to the company. The American Management Association estimates that a company pays about one year's salary to replace a mid-level manager who quits, when recruitment, selection, and training costs are totaled for the new hire.

The third way they sacrifice to their management by terror is that they lose control over their reputations and professional options. When a boss fails to inspire loyalty and respect among the workforce, his or her own prospects for professional advancement begin to dim. This is not to say that jerks never receive promotions. On balance, however, managers are judged by what they inspire in others. If their legacy is only a mixture of fear and hatred, any board or corporate leader would think twice before handing over the reins of supervision to such an individual.

The Nice Boss Made Me Do It

On the flip side, some employees act and speak disingenuously because they don't want to disappoint a boss who has been kind, understanding, and solicitous of their professional welfare. A hotel manager in Florida tells such a story:

> The hotel chain is privately owned by a gentleman in his early eighties. When I say "gentleman," I'm choosing exactly the right word. He has been practically like a father to me and to the rest of the managers in his hotels. He wants to be proud of us and regularly sends a bottle of champagne to my office when he hears about something good that has happened at the hotel. But he's such a gentle, sweet guy

that a lot of managers—including myself at times—don't get around to telling him less than good news.

For example, I've got a mess right now in my hotel because I fired a minority employee. She's claiming that race was a factor in the firing. I know I ought to tell the hotel owner about the situation, but I don't want to disappoint the old guy or have him feel that I have let him down in some way. This is just one example. At his other hotels, there are plenty of cases of negative occurrences that any owner would want and need to know about. But because he has been so kind and trusting toward his managers, we've developed kind of a don't ask/don't tell policy toward him. It's almost as if we're trying to protect him against anything that would disturb him—but not because we're afraid of him. Much the opposite. We love the guy and just don't want to let him down. In the meantime, though, a number of serious problems are piling up at all the hotels—things an owner should be involved in. One of these days the dam is going to break and all the bad news will come flooding out. Sometimes I think it would be better if he wasn't so nice all the time so we managers could feel okay about sharing bad news as well as good news.

The phenomenon of the manager who shuts down employee candor through kindness and courtesy is less common but just as serious as the ranting boss who manages through scare tactics. The employee of a "loving" boss also experiences a powerful form of fear—the fear of losing the boss's regard and affection. Somewhere in their relationship the message was never sent or received that the boss's good feelings aren't going to evaporate just because an employee candidly shared bad news, an unpopular idea, or a problem of some kind.

Peers That Threaten Candor

Vivian, a California department manager in a large clothing store, talks about the problem of peer relations in the workplace.

I manage Young Women's Wear in a national chain department store. It's hard to explain, but I feel like I'm always looking over my shoulder to keep track of what Rachel is doing in her department (Formal Wear), Alphonse in his (Men's Suits), and all the rest in the store. There's a constant bickering match going on among managers that has nothing to do with the manager, who kind of leaves us all alone to do our thing. Take stocking, for example. When boxes arrive to be unpacked, there are a few hours when my clerks are out there with boxes in the aisles doing the work of getting the clothes on shelves and hangers. But if those boxes are in the aisle longer than about two hours, Rachel will start gossiping to other managers about how I don't run a tight ship in my department. She should talk! I saw two of her clerks come in at least half an hour late a couple days ago. Rachel didn't discipline them at all. My clerks get to work right on time or they hear about it from me. Alphonse is always looking over at my department and rolling his eyes when he sees any of us sitting down instead of standing up. He makes all his sales people stand up even when no customers are in the department. I told him that some of my people have physical issues and have to avoid being on their feet all day. What I said was less than candid, but it got him off my back, at least for now.

In Vivian's case, peer pressure exerts a powerful influence over what she says and does during the business day. At some companies, peer pressure discourages rate-busting, that is, when one employee works hard and ends up producing more than his or her peers. This work achievement unfortunately makes peers appear, by contrast, to be somehow inferior or lazy. In this kind of environment, top performers quickly find themselves alienated and isolated from their peer group; lunch invitations dry up, coffee breaks are solo occasions, and the offending performer is not included in workplace jokes and banter. Through such social punishment, the person is taught not to work so quickly or so well. Put another way, peers let it be known (and felt) that they don't trust a star.

At other companies, the culture enforces a code of silence, most familiar, perhaps, from the countless movies and TV shows depicting such a code within police departments. Employees in such a corporate culture hold themselves back from any initiative or original thinking. They are tight-lipped, sticking only to basic job requirements. "Move that box" means precisely that in the code of silence culture. It does not mean, "Let me know if you see that the box is leaking" or "Be extra careful because the box contains fragile items." In this business environment, employees have no trust in management. They don't even think of contributing good ideas for work improvement, letting the boss know how or why a problem occurred, or asking for more responsibility than the boss has already assigned.

Client Pressures on Candor

Clients can have a similar influence on a worker's core candor.

> It was a huge account, [recalls a Minnesota manager,] the largest of my career. I didn't want anything to go wrong—and when it did, I didn't want the client to know about the problems. I'll admit that I was less than candid at times in my efforts to reassure the client. If a shipment was late, I said the truck was involved in a minor accident. If a progress report wasn't received by the client, I blamed a computer problem. At the time, I knew I wasn't being candid, but felt that I was saying these things from the best of motives—trying to keep an important client happy. If a problem occurred that I couldn't easily explain away by making up a likely story, I just avoided phone calls from the client. Better to say nothing, I figured, than to be put on the spot. I was afraid that if the client knew how often my company dropped the ball, he would lose confidence in my firm and me. What else could I do? Like I said, it was a huge account. I had to treat it that way.

Client problems are often described as a one-way street with the company playing the role of villain and the client as victim. In this version of things, the company sends false signals or incorrect products or faulty services to the client, who in turn is disappointed and angry. But those roles can also be reversed: the client can be the "bad guy" pressuring the company or its agents to say and do things they would prefer not to.

Take Wendell's dilemma at Henderson Publishing. The company creates and distributes medical textbooks. Wendell is thrilled when he receives an order of six hundred books from a large East Coast medical school. At $180 per book, it's a worthwhile sale for the company and a healthy commission for Wendell. He is less thrilled, however, when the business agent for the medical school reaches him by phone.

"You got our order?" the agent asks.

"Yes," Wendell says. "Thanks very much. The order will ship within forty-eight hours."

"Well," the agent hesitates, "we need to talk first."

"What do you mean?" Wendell asks innocently.

"You know," the agent hints. "An add-on. A perk."

"You want to add something to your order?" Wendell questions, still not understanding.

"You're going to make me spell it out?" The agent laughs sarcastically. "I want a couple laptops."

"Uh, we don't sell laptops." The general drift of the conversation was starting to occur to Wendell.

"Yeah, two laptops. I figure it like this. Our order amounts to more than $100,000 to your company. Your commission is what, $15,000 or so? Laptops are only about $900 each these days. I want two of them. They can be sent directly to my home. I'll give you the address."

"That's not our policy . . ." Wendell starts to explain.

"Then you're the only publisher who doesn't do it," snaps the agent. "I can make sure the order goes someplace else."

You can guess how this situation played out. Wendell took the issue to his boss who, eager to make her numbers for the quarter, told Wendell she would split the cost of the two laptops with him. She expressed her opinion that the company wasn't doing anything terribly wrong. There was no law against donating a couple laptops to a reputable medical school, even if they were sent to the business agent's home.

"Besides," Wendell's boss concludes, "nine hundred bucks each is a pretty cheap discount in consideration of how much you and I stand to make on this sale. And if we treat them right with these laptops, they'll probably come back to us next semester."

Both Wendell and his boss agreed to keep the matter between them. No need to alert Mr. Henderson, the publisher and owner of the company.

Many negotiations of this sort pass unnoticed. This one didn't. A year after delivering the laptops to the agent's home, Wendell and his boss received a subpoena to testify in a fraud case brought by the medical school against its business manager. He had been dipping generously into many of the school's large-dollar orders. If convicted, he was going to jail.

Mr. Henderson, the company owner, found out about the scandal and his company's part in it. He promptly fired Wendell and Wendell's boss.

Customers can exert excruciating pressure on company representatives to break trust with their company leaders. In these situations, candor can save the day in terms of one's career and the welfare of the company.

Immediately report the bribe, extortion, or other impropriety to your manager. If he or she steers you wrong (as in the case of Wendell's boss), take the issue higher in the company. Don't fall for the Nuremburg defense idea—"I'm not guilty because I was just doing what my boss told me to do."

Call the customer's bluff. Demands for unauthorized considerations and side deals are often as dangerous for the client as they are for your company. Just say no, politely and firmly, as countless American firms have had to do with international buyers and sellers who fully expect large payoffs and bribes to accompany their deals.

Talk through the issue with the customer. Explain that your company prohibits such arrangements and that you will get in serious trouble if you participate as the client wishes. Reasoned dialogue can often help a client see the situation in a clearer light.

Chapter Six

Struggles for Trust
The Personal Dimension

"The best way to find out if you can trust somebody is to trust them."
                                                    Ernest Hemingway

If a picture is worth a thousand words, a story must be worth at least twice the number of words it takes to tell. A story can provide subtleties and shadings that never show up in lists of principles and theories, particularly where human protagonists are involved. The following three scenarios draw together details from the lives of many professional people; no one individual is featured here, and any similarity to the life or experience of one person is purely coincidental.

Please read the first scenario with an eye toward one question: what would I have done under the circumstances? Vic, our main character in the story, faces personal and professional trust challenges. You may agree or disagree with the choices he makes, but in either case, take a moment to think through his options. If he had made different choices, what would the likely consequences have been? Where did he go wrong? What can he do? By answering these questions about a fictional character, you prepare yourself to find similar answers for real-life trust dilemmas.

Scenario 1: The Change

6:30 AM. Vic used to need an alarm clock. Now his body clock predictably rouses him within a few minutes of wake-up time. Not always happily. He pulls the covers back and lies still for a couple of minutes before beginning the day. His wife snoozes peacefully beside him. A wall away his two preschoolers continue their deep slumber without a peep.

Home in the morning. He yawns and stretches his arms back toward the headboard. How different, Vic thinks, from the nutty work world he will be walking into an hour from now. The office will start to wake up by 8 AM and reach full roar by 8:30—e-mail popping, bosses complaining, secretaries juggling a dozen tasks, voicemail piling up.

Vic knows that sometime between now and when he arrives for work he will go through what his coworkers at the office humorously call "the change." He will suit up literally and metaphorically to play the game of business yet another day. Dr. Jekyll and Mr. Hyde. He never feels entirely comfortable in that suit, at least not the kind of comfort he feels here at 6:35 in the morning, with the family still asleep. Vic shakes off sleep and steps into a hot shower.

"Morning, honey," his wife calls. She is already in the kitchen. Sometimes he beats her downstairs and makes breakfast for the gang himself. The two kids sit plopped at the table awaiting their usual of cereal and orange juice. The ritual of hugging Daddy takes just a few seconds, but it seems to start everyone's day off on the right foot.

"Billy, will you pass me the cornflakes?" Vic asks. The big red "Cornflakes" stares at him from across the table. His mind flips forward to business again for a split second. Here at the breakfast table everything is exactly as it seems. Cornflakes are cornflakes. Milk is milk. Billy wouldn't pass him the Captain Crunch and pretend it was cornflakes. He certainly wouldn't say something noncommittal like, "I will look into passing the cornflakes and get back to you." Things have names that everyone agrees upon. People do the common-sense right thing without thinking twice.

How different from the deceptive dance and stalling lingo he will be engaged in when he gets to work in an hour or so: "team synergy," "customer service," "fulfilling the mission," "exceeding expectations," "living the vision." His boss likes those words and likes Vic to use them as well. All the fast-track mid-level managers talk a good game using such phrases. But who knows what that gobbledygook means? How did you know when you had it or did it or needed it? It wasn't as plain and simple as "Pass the cornflakes." A lot of terms in business don't seem to have anything behind them. And some things have no names.

Vic pours a full bowl of cornflakes and trickles on some milk. "Susie, I'll pick you up from dance lessons right at 5 o'clock, okay?" His daughter nods yes and goes back to stirring the cereal, fruit, and milk as rapidly as possible without spilling.

What a great feeling, Vic thinks to himself, making a commitment you really mean to keep. She and I just agreed on what's going to happen. She knows I will be there at five and so do I. At least half the time at work we sit around and agree on what's going to happen. Then we go our separate ways and nothing happens, or the wrong thing happens. We never really mean what we say. Vic looks at his watch. In less than an hour I'll be at work making commitments that I know I won't be able or willing to keep. Just part of the game there. Say anything, do what you want, don't get jammed up.

He feels his mood darken in contrast to the lighthearted jabber around the breakfast table. He snaps back from thinking about work, work, work and looks at his wife and kids.

"What's your day like?" he asks his wife, Linda, a freelance graphics designer.

"Busier than yours," she smiles. "I've got a conference call this morning to bid a job for those real-estate brochures I told you about. Then this afternoon I guess I'll work on a couple Web site designs until the kids get home from school."

Vic silently wishes he worked the way Linda does. She gives straight answers to him, to herself, and to her clients: no baloney, no white lies, no creative excuses. She just speaks candidly. Vic envies her.

What a difference at his job. If he had asked the same question, "What's your day like?", to his coworkers, they would bristle defensively. "Just the usual B.S.," some of them would say. Others, particularly his subordinates, would make up a manure pile of false activities just to cover themselves. His fellow managers would turn the question back on him: "Why are you asking? Did someone tell you to check on me? What's with all these questions?"

Vic grabs a few breakfast dishes and begins tucking them into the dishwasher. Bottom line, he ponders to himself, home is an honest place where people can tell it like it is. Work is often a dishonest place where people are on guard about what they say or just remain silent out of fear of saying anything at all. They fabricate excuses and stories without thinking twice. Getting candor from someone at work is rare indeed.

Vic waves goodbye to the family and turns the ignition key in his car. "The adventure continues," he groans to himself as he backs out of the driveway and heads toward the freeway for the umpteenth time on his way to work. Familiar landmarks flash by across the windshield. He plays around with a quirky idea. Where exactly on the way to work—this block? the next? a mile down the freeway?—does he go through "the change" from Vic the Honest Family Guy to Vic the Tricky Work Guy, the guy who is capable of looking a client in the eye and promising a delivery date that has no chance of materializing. The guy who unashamedly blames his failure to produce a client letter on time on network problems and lost voicemail. The guy who has learned how to lay low in meetings, saying just enough to create the impression of participation. And Vic was one of the good guys—a fast-tracker tabbed for promotion in a year or so. Imagine the cynics in the company!

Vic steers onto an off-ramp for the last ten minutes of his drive to the office. The thought won't go away. Vic wonders half aloud why he can't be the same guy at work he is at the breakfast table back home. And if he has to change his standards and ethics when he steps into the office, what prevents those twisted morals from coming home with him? At what point will he start making promises to his kids without ever intending to keep them? At what point will it be as easy to kiss off candor to Linda as it is to his boss, coworkers, and clients? And when will he get so turned around with his own lack of candor that he won't be able to distinguish fact from fantasy in any aspect of his life?

Vic honks at a car that cuts in too close ahead of him. A lack of candor is a good way to say it. He doesn't tell his boss that black is white. Vic thinks for a moment. Gray is the problem. Everything at work shifts toward gray. You are never sure what started out as white or black. People, from the top boss to the lowest staffer, guard their words and only let out small bursts of occasional candor. They speak about what makes them look good and hide the rest of the story.

It wasn't supposed to turn out this way. Vic thought he had shaken off the gray of mixed and messed-up messages when he changed jobs from MegaGroup Health Insurance to his present employer, Greenline Health Network. As a graduate fresh out of a high-minded MBA program (*two* courses in business ethics!), Vic had taken a good-paying mid-level managerial job with the corporate giant MegaGroup without really getting to know the company. He simply knew they were huge in the marketplace and generous with top-performing managers.

He worked hard at MegaGroup—too hard for his own good, one boss told him. As an economic analyst, Vic dug into the core statistics that made MegaGroup tick, but he felt increasingly sick at what he discovered. MegaGroup, it turned out, was in the business of offering low health insurance rates to large companies, then doing everything possible within the small print of policies to turn down medical claims from clients. The company's percentage of approved claims, Vic learned to his chagrin, was the lowest in the insurance industry. Vic began to feel that the company was a crook and that he was driving the getaway car.

With his wife's encouragement and support, Vic began looking for an insurance company with a more humane, honest vision and a more compassionate face for the public. He interviewed at five companies before discovering a smaller company, Greenline Health Network, that seemed to fit his career bill to a tee. This firm was proud of the fact that it spent more on the hiring and training of their customer representatives ("customer care specialists," they called themselves) than any other comparably sized insurance company. When you called Greenline, Vic found, you could be assured that you wouldn't be talking to a claims agent with "attitude" or with someone intent on being your antagonist throughout the claims process.

Greenline actually had a program for bringing skilled mothers—women who knew what it meant to care—back into the workplace. One of the company's ads, in fact, touted the gentle patience of their customer reps: "When you feel like talking to Mom, it's time to call Greenline." A bit too sugary for some, but a real hit in the market, especially with mid- to lower-income populations. "I'm so sorry for what you've been through," reps were trained to say, "and I'll do everything I can to move your claim along quickly."

Vic was doing well at Greenline after four years and had received hints from company executives about a big promotion in his future. He just had to be careful not to step out of line, not to fail at something too noticeably or even succeed too visibly in a way that made his bosses look lazy. Sure he had ideas for improvement and a keen eye for untangling work problems, but he had learned to stifle, to repress his ideas. Why make someone else look bad? Greenline was all about "no ripples." Too many good waves were as dangerous to a career as too many bad waves. Vic had learned not to rock the boat.

It's not just me, Vic consoles himself. It's everyone at work.

We get used to clamming up about what we really think. We end up saying what the other person wants to hear.

He looks for his favorite parking place in the company lot. Found it! Since he got his favorite spot, Vic figures it will be a reasonably good day. His good omen, he calls it.

That happy illusion is shattered by the first phone call he receives when he sits down at his desk. "Vic," wheezes a pinched male voice on the other end, "this is Frederick in Forecasting. I need the 7064-A report from you by 10:15 tomorrow morning. This is urgent. In fact, I would say very urgent."

"Yeah, Frederick, 10:15. Right."

"So I can expect it on my desk no later than 10:15 tomorrow?"

"Sounds fine with me." Vic chooses his words carefully. Frederick isn't his boss and all this "urgent" stuff is probably just a figment of Frederick's imagination. Vic certainly isn't going to let himself be managed by Frederick. This character is a hyper-diaper kind of guy—rigid timelines and schedules, carefully constructed work plans stretching out several months in advance, and a Gestapo way of relating to others in the company. Frederick keeps a personal calendar broken into fifteen-minute increments and fills it out in elaborate detail for many weeks into the future. The office joke is that Frederick even calendars times for making love to his wife—and that the fifteen-minute slot is too long.

Vic hangs up the phone and feels the familiar fog of the workday begin to settle over him. He is on the other side of "the change." Cornflakes aren't cornflakes anymore. Now it depends on who wants them, when, and why. An agreed-upon deadline isn't really a deadline and isn't actually agreed to. Fog everywhere. Besides, uptight jerks like Frederick almost force a guy to forget candor, or at least make up phony stories and excuses, Vic tells himself.

In actuality, Vic has no intention of completing or even starting the 7064-A report by 10:15 tomorrow. He will do it when he feels like it. And he already is thinking ahead to how he will answer Frederick's frantic phone call tomorrow: "Gee, Frederick, my boss put me on a high-priority project that we have to finish up right away. But I'll get that report over to you in a couple days. Sorry. Yeah, I know it was urgent. You told me. A couple days. Look, Frederick, I hear you. But that's the best I can do. It was an emergency. Got to go."

Great thing about the word "couple"—does it mean two, three, or even four or more? He isn't going to let Frederick pin him down. If the office nagster has the nerve to call him again, Vic will remind him, "Frederick, I said a couple days. That doesn't necessarily mean two, no matter what your calendar or dictionary says. I'll call you when the report is ready." Click.

Sure, Vic knows, it is doublespeak, but it is the only way to survive in a world of Fredericks and their strict schedules. Everyone does it at work. Vic knows he can't expect a straight yes or no from anyone in the office, much less his boss. That's why work teams are such a dismal waste of time at Greenline. No one really speaks up to tell others candidly what is going on. As a consequence, teams end up taking forever to complete work that one person could have done in half the time.

Over coffee, Vic has a standard challenge for any of his manager friends: Go down the hall and ask a straightforward work question to the first person you meet. The typical answers to any questions or concerns, Vic claims, will likely be, "Let me check on that" or "I'll get back to you" or "We're having a meeting on that in a few days." "Pass the cornflakes" never brought the cornflakes any closer at work.

Vic knows that if the boss or a coworker gives a straight, non-evasive answer, then that person will be on the spot to actually come through on his or her commitment. Candor invites a lot of notoriety and some heavy lifting as follow-up work. Not to act on the basis of your straight-from-the-hip words reveals a person to be a hypocrite or a phony. No one at work wants those labels hung around their neck. So they tiptoe around the edges of candor, saying just enough to get a colleague or client off their back while not firming up any particular course of action or specific performance. Welcome to the world of gray.

The next bump in Vic's day comes when his boss sends him the long-dreaded e-mail about an upcoming business trip to Houston over the weekend. It's summer and must be 95 degrees in the shade with 90 percent humidity, Vic frets to himself. There's no way I'm going on this trip if I can wriggle out of it.

Vic, a long way now from the guy at home who called cornflakes, cornflakes, begins to consider his options for avoiding the uncomfortable business trip. Some cock and bull story about a health problem isn't the way to go—the boss might require a note from Vic's doctor. And Vic doesn't want to get the reputation around the office of being an invalid of some kind. Nor can he make up some story about an important project he is working on. The boss knows his work activities and has the option of redefining priorities in favor of the sweat bath in Houston.

Vic searches his bag of tricks without thinking twice about the man who woke up next to his wife this morning. A lack of candor is no problem if it bails him out of this Houston thing. Vic knows that the office culture generally looks with sympathy on any employee facing the loss of a loved one or an impending operation for a spouse or child. Vic hasn't plucked this string since last year, when he covered an unscheduled day off with a story about his grandmother's health emergency. (Well, she *was* in a rest home. How would anyone in the company discover that she was doing just fine there?)

He pecked a message at his keyboard back to his boss: "I feel terrible about this, but we need to find someone else who's available for the Houston trip because . . ." Here's where Vic needs a good story. Not a candid one necessarily, but one that has an air of candor, like most messages in the company. A story that sounds real and can't be easily checked by anyone in the company. A story that will lead any compassionate manager to conclude, "Well, we can't send Vic. He's facing a hard situation with one of his kids."

Vic looks out the window and tries not to think of the world where trees are trees, cornflakes are cornflakes, and what a person says has some reasonable verisimilitude to the way things are. He is looking out the window searching for a passable fantasy.

"We need to find someone else who's available for the Houston trip," Vic finally keys in, "because my youngest daughter needs to see a specialist this weekend. The doctor wants both parents there in case we need to be tested. Maybe a genetic thing of some kind. The doctor fit us in on this coming Saturday, and if we don't keep this appointment, it may be months before he has another opening. I'm really stuck. I would gladly go on this trip if I could. In fact, I was looking forward to it."

The ruse works. An hour later the boss sends a terse e-mail letting Vic know that he is off the hook for the trip. A junior employee, Alice, loses the draw of straws and is drafted in Vic's place. She pops by Vic's office to express her sympathy about his daughter's sudden illness and to ask how the child is doing. Vic puts on an appropriate expression of angst and extends his story a bit: "She's had these weak spells and nausea. Our primary care doc can't figure out what's going on so he's sending us to a specialist. Thanks for your concern—and I really appreciate you taking my place on the Houston trip. I owe you one."

Vic takes a midmorning bathroom break and catches his image in the mirror. He looks okay, he judges. He still appears to be a bright guy worthy of promotion. He straightens his tie. He is looking at a guy who knows how the work world works: what to say, what not to say, how to make up whatever line you need to smooth over problems and keep yourself smelling like a rose. One of his buddies in the company calls him "the Artful Dodger." They both have had a good laugh over the nickname. Best of all, he isn't going to Houston.

Almost noon. Another corporate day half over without much to show for it except a couple of empty cups of coffee. At twelve sharp all managers, including Vic, have to show up in the main cafeteria for a working lunch featuring a televised "speech to the troops" from the Greenline CEO, Gwen Richards. Richards champions the kinder, gentler approach to health insurance interaction with clients. As an EVP prior to becoming CEO, she spoke out on what valued customers see and feel in contacts with Greenline and showed the way to what she called "profitability and responsibility with a heart." She practically wrote the mission and vision statement for the company single-handedly. The message had worked not only in the marketplace—Greenline continued to grow at a 12 percent clip in each of the following four years—it had also worked to attract people like Vic to the company as key employees.

The men and women now seated around Vic in the crowded cafeteria share a common desire to work for a company with a sense of ethics, even at salaries that are somewhat less than those paid by corporate giants like MegaGroup. Vic vividly recalls the gratified smile on his wife's face when she saw a Greenline ad on TV showing an elderly customer being treated with patience and dignity by a thoroughly trained customer service representative. "That's your company," she murmured to Vic.

A sudden hush falls over the cafeteria as the lights dim and the CEO's face looms large on three closed-circuit TV screens. Gwen Richards begins with a forgettable joke about her similarities to Katie Couric, then launches into the pitch that has made her a legend in the company and increasingly in the insurance industry: "Those of you seeing my face and hearing my voice today are the true corporate champions I want to salute. You have believed in the Greenline vision of a new level and a new spirit of customer service. You have taken that vision into every contact with our 11 million customers. Today your attention to the needs of each one of these customers has earned you (Gwen pauses dramatically) the Malcolm Baldridge Customer Service Award." A large trophy appears next to her on screen. She puts her hand on it as if patting the head of a child. A scattering of applause percolates throughout the audience, tentative at first but then rising to a hearty crescendo. She continues, "This award recognizes what we as a company have done well so far and challenges us to do even better in the years ahead."

Vic returns from his working lunch feeling reasonably proud of himself and his company. He made the right move, he decides, in going with Greenline instead of staying with MegaGroup, salary levels notwithstanding. He can sleep better at night knowing that the public likes his company. Borrowing an old cliché from an insurance competitor, he feels he is "in good hands" at Greenline.

He settles into his desk chair and begins thumbing somewhat randomly through a pile of data sheets that will eventually become the 7064-A report that Frederick was pestering him about. Vic wonders if the figures will tell the same odd story this year as last. Some "quirky anomaly," he told his boss at the time.

Vic runs a few quick calculations to get a trend line for the current data. Digits flash on the spreadsheet like fruit images on a slot machine, but the thrust of the data is becoming clear. What Vic sees on his computer screen chills any last embers of warmth from Gwen Richards' glowing speech of congratulations. There before him, in rough but essentially accurate form, is a statistical tale that the Malcolm Baldridge Award evaluators apparently didn't get to see. After all the hoopla of "compassionate, understanding customer care specialists" at Greenline, the actual rate of approval for medical claims is not significantly higher than at his last company, the knee-jerk claim rejecters at MegaGroup.

Vic pushes himself back in his chair and lets out a low whistle. Gwen Richards has pulled off a sleight of hand worthy of

Houdini. While customers are basking in the interpersonal warmth of their customer care, they aren't really paying attention to the fact that their claims are being turned down in massive and, for the company, profitable numbers. Turned down sweetly, of course. Turned down after "taking this claim immediately to my supervisor to see if we can't do something for you, Mrs. Jones." Turned down after getting to know the client and listening patiently to his stories of war injuries from Korea and discomfort from a trick knee ("Mr. Conroy, my uncle had exactly the same kind of knee problem. He never knew when it was going out on him.") Trained to say soothing things as often as necessary to anesthetize clients against the pain of having medical claims rejected. Yada-yada-yada, as Seinfeld would say.

But shrewd yada. Vic recognizes that Gwen Richards has poured an immense amount of money into corporate training to field an impressive corps of customer service reps who know how to nurture their customers into meek submission. Too many clients never got their legitimate claims approved and paid—but never complained. They felt that they had been treated so nicely. The customer service rep had been so understanding. She said she would do everything she could. As one woman told the Malcolm Baldridge Award interviewers, "The woman I talked to at Greenline explained to me how hard she was working on my claim and how many doctors had to review it. They all had to agree, she said, and that took time. It didn't turn out the way I wanted, but I can't blame her. She was on my side from the beginning and did everything she could to help me. She must have called me back five or six times to keep me up to date on her progress. Once we talked for forty-five minutes, even about her kids and mine. That's what I call excellent customer service."

Vic piles the data pages neatly to one side of his desk. No wonder Frederick is so eager to get his hands on the 7064-A report. Frederick will massage the numbers so that they eventually match the company image and public vision. It won't be hard. Vic knows the statistical tricks: simply invent an elaborate appeals process and subtract out a healthy percentage of rejected claims, redefining them as pending and therefore off the books as far as the actual claim rejection rate goes. Voila, a company that practices what it preaches. All legal and all highly confidential.

Vic twiddles his key chain, contemplating some way to take off early for the day and go home. No convincing excuse comes to mind, especially since he needs to be a good boy around the office while the boss settles down about the whole Houston business trip thing. Vic thinks about sharing the data results with his wife when he gets home. Linda would catch onto the company's deception right away. But why tell her, he mulls. She admires the company I work for and thinks well of me for working here instead of at MegaGroup. I get nods of approval whenever we go out and someone asks where I work. Everybody likes the Greenline TV ads. If Gwen Richards can pull the wool over the customers' eyes, I guess I can too.

Let's reflect briefly on Vic's situation. In part of his life—the important part, as far as he is concerned—he feels that he acts with complete candor. He likes the feelings that such candor brings. He likes the trust relationships that such candor encourages. It feels good for Vic to be absolutely straight with his wife and kids. He knows who he is at home.

His work life, by contrast, is a complicated web of distrust based largely on a lack of candor at all levels. Vic trusts no one at work. Because he has little respect for Frederick and the rest of his colleagues, he feels no pang of conscience when he bends candor to the breaking point in his excuses, stories, and waffling. As a rising manager, he begins to view a lack of candor as the art of war in the hard world of business.

And he's winning that war, by all appearances. He's making a decent salary and moving ahead faster than most in the company. His wife is proud of him for working for a humane corporation.

So what's the problem? Vic convinces himself that he is satisfied with the person he is at work although it's quite a different person than he is at home. He observes that he puts candor on and off like a suit of business clothes. Nothing is wrong, he tells himself. Yet something feels wrong.

As you contemplate Vic's story, try to reach your own conclusions about the role of candor in private and professional life. Can each of us go through "the change" each day on the way to work? Are there consequences for our personal lives, our sense of self, and perhaps our professional prospects as well?

Scenario 2: What Happened to Our Innovators?

In the following story, trust relationships begin to fail not because of any one individual's purposeful lack of candor but of flawed relationships forced on employees by the company's approach to rapid growth. As trust among individuals fades, so does the spirit of innovation on which the company was founded.

"Whirlwind" hardly describes the last two years for Richard Eastwood, Linda Ortiz, and Sam Foster, former MBA classmates at State U. Toward the end of their academic program, they got together over a beer one memorable evening to share a common desire: to break the mold and do something entrepreneurial with their lives. That evening's impassioned conversation lasted until the wee hours, ending in a firm commitment by each of the three newly minted partners to make it happen.

"It was literally the best of times," recalls Linda Ortiz. "We were communicating with one another almost constantly in person, by e-mail, or over the phone. If I had a hot idea, it was my natural first instinct to share it with Richard and Sam even before I figured out the best way to express it. We bounced ideas back and forth until they took shape as something we could use. Everything in those days was rapid-fire. We had to get right to the point because we didn't want to waste valuable time. Our product needed to be first to market for success, not a second or third wave 'me too' item."

The product quickly took the form of a retail line of sunglasses, "StandOuts," as they were called in the accompanying advertising and marketing campaign. These sunglasses have the optical distinction of masking virtually all colors except the one color most desired by the wearer. For example, tennis players choose the Tennis StandOut model because it highlights anything yellow in the field of vision, including yellow tennis balls. Park rangers love the Color StandOut glasses, which mask green (including bushes and trees) to highlight reds, blues, and other primary colors, the shirt colors, for example, of a lost hiker. Skiers favor the NoBlind model, which cancels the effects of snow blindness and highlights defining shades of gray and blue on the slopes.

"One ferocious argument we had," Sam recounts, "was over the status aspects of our product. At first we couldn't agree on whether we were marketing to upper-income people with a lot of discretionary income, such as skiers and tennis players, or whether we should open up our technology to ordinary occupations and trades. Richard said absolutely not; it would wreck our image. Linda was just as adamant on the other side. She said we should sell our product anywhere it could be useful. I was on the fence for a while, but eventually leaned to Linda's position and together we drew Richard, kicking and screaming, to our point of view."

The result was a separate product line, Work StandOuts, featuring sunglasses adjusted to the needs of particular occupations. Hundreds of thousands of pairs sold to one major corporation that needed to focus on specific color patterns for quality control on the production line. Thousands more went to agri-businesses, particularly for fruit and vegetable harvesters who needed a certain color to stand out—red, let's say, in the case of apples—for a thorough picking. Many growers reported a 15 percent increase in their harvest due to Work StandOuts; their pickers now weren't overlooking fruit hidden on the trees.

Flash forward three years. Standout Optics is now a publicly traded company with more than eighteen hundred employees in four states. Production of the sunglass lenses is handled entirely in China through a subcontractor.

Richard Eastwood remembers the growth process. "After our second round of funding, it quickly got so that Linda, Sam, and I couldn't handle the crush of daily business while we were also busy expanding our product line, nailing down our patents, doing trade shows, and creating advertising. We figured we needed a first lieutenant of sorts to take the pressure off us and free us up for some of the big-picture tasks we faced. Without taking the military metaphor seriously, we actually did end up hiring a retired army major with a lot of experience in organizing projects, keeping schedules, and running a tight personnel ship. When Bill Henry came aboard, we all breathed a sigh of relief. He seemed ready and able to handle the day-to-day headaches of product development, delivery, and customer relations. We gave him a free hand to hire the people he needed to spread our business at first across the Western states and eventually nationwide."

Linda laughs. "Bill was a bit of a character, especially when we first met him. He said 'sir' and 'ma'am' to us and would only disagree with us when we told him to do so. As he put it, we were the generals and he was there to carry out the mission. Richard, Sam, and I sat in on some of his first hiring sessions, but after a while the personnel needs of the company became so great that we just let Bill handle it. He quickly hired an HR person and she ended up doing most of the actual recruiting and interviews. Before we knew it, we had more than a hundred employees (now it's eighteen hundred!) and an actual organization chart on Bill's office wall showing who reported to whom in an elaborate series of lines."

"We're making money," Richard concedes, with a look of concern and perplexity on his face, "but I don't know . . . Something seems to be changing in the way the company feels. It's like we're settling into middle age."

"I know what you mean," Sam concurs. "Everyone is doing their job, but the fire is definitely not burning in the belly anymore for 95 percent of the people in the company. It's getting to feel like working at the post office."

"So," Linda joins in, "where did the fire go? God knows we had it when we were praying for that first round of venture capital funding. And remember how thrilled we were when Rite Aid gave us our first contract for a few thousand pairs of glasses? We sell hundreds of thousands of pairs now. Pictures of our sunglasses are in every magazine. And our employees seem to yawn about it all."

"Yeah," Richard replies, "when was the last time we got an unsolicited idea from one of our employees for an improvement of some kind in the product or a new spin-off product of some kind? That's the kind of thinking we did every single day in the beginning: what's new, what's hot, what hasn't been tried? I don't blame Bill; he certainly organized us at a time when we desperately needed some organization around here. But little by little things seemed to slip downhill as we brought more people into the company."

Linda pauses, then sits back in her chair as if hit by a gust of wind. "OMG, as my daughter says. Guys, I think the light just came on about what's been happening here."

"Do share," Sam says with a smile.

"Look," Linda begins. "When we started this company, it was just the three of us. We could say anything to one another. We had no fear about asking any question or making any suggestion. In a way, that slowed us down because we got bogged down by tangents and dead-end discussions. But we enjoyed the back and forth, and as we talked more and more, we trusted each other more and more. We knew we would make mistakes together, but we never doubted each other's total commitment to making this work."

Linda continues, "Do you remember how we had to coax Bill Henry into disagreeing with us or suggesting anything new? I love Bill, but his idea of innovation is making the trains run faster on time. He always says that we are the creative ones. Well, that's the organization Bill has built so well for us. Damn, he's good. But we know we need the ideas of our folks closest to the customers and the kids we just hired whose brains have not been numbed by corporate life."

"That's not the organization Bill built, and we supported his building it," Richard chimes in. "He built an organization incredibly strong on execution. I am continually amazed at how Bill and his people spot inefficiencies every day in our operations. Bill's got his eye on everything from logistics to manufacturing to delivery to display cases. He outsourced most of our human resources function and no one complained."

"That's pretty accurate," Sam says, "but maybe we did not get any complaints about HR because our people are not used to or not given the chance to give feedback or criticize company moves. It's hard to imagine going from a hands-on HR rep to a recorded telephone system and Web site for HR without one complaint from over a thousand employees. The new HR system just cannot be that good. I have never even used the new system. Bill just sits down with me, we chat about the options, and he takes care of it for me."

Linda and Richard stare at each other as the same light bulb goes off in their heads. Linda blurts out, "Bill built a 'Yes sir/Yes ma'am' organization for us, a bunch of freethinkers. He's got his people so focused on delivering on their target goals that they cannot see the big picture. They don't get it that someone very soon will figure out how to make better or cooler or higher contrast sunglasses than us. And probably cheaper! And, our people don't get that the three of us—the founders—are too distant from customers and retail stores carrying our products to know what to do next."

Richard concludes, "It's time for Bill Henry to take a long vacation. We need him to keep the trains running on time, but we need to energize our people. We've got to get out and visit our employees and let them know we want their ideas and suggestions. We want to hear what's going badly and what's going well. We need all people to know that we trust them to work hard and to think and ask questions. We need them to put us on the spot about why we are basically still selling the same sunglasses after two years of full production. We need them to help us figure out where the next train is headed."

What happens to candor—and the courage to offer innovative ideas—in an organization where getting the trains to run on time is more important than where the trains are headed?

1. Employees get used to parking their brains at the door when they step into the office. Employees fully capable of offering valuable opinions, feedback, and insight are regularly stifled by the spoken or unspoken message, "Just do your job. You're not here to make waves. If you have suggestions, submit them to your supervisor."
2. Innovation in this kind of environment falls to a select few in R&D, or the company's brilliant founders in this case, rather than being the common interest of employees at all levels. For example, a salesperson listening to customers' reactions to the company's sunglasses is in an excellent position to gather ideas of what people like, what they don't like, and what they wish for in the product. But back at the office that salesperson gets squashed: "Yeah, yeah, you talked to some customers. Good for you, good for them. Look, your job is selling. Upstairs there are lots of white collars doing marketing studies and all that. There's a reason they're upstairs and we're down here. Get it?"

Even if employees are not lectured in this way, they nevertheless get the idea from company culture that their bright ideas are not welcome.

3. Communications at all levels are written merely to satisfy, not to exceed or surprise. When writing a report on a recent visit to retail locations selling their line of sunglasses, an employee simply asks, "What does my supervisor want to see in this report?" That becomes the candor boundary for communication—and may as well be a twenty-foot fence. If that employee ran across a startling new item on the market and a possible competitor to the company's products, it's unlikely that such vital news would appear in the trip report. "Just tell me where you went, how much you spent, and who you saw," the supervisor yawns.

4. "What is" quickly metamorphoses into "What should be." On the first few days at the job, bright people may feel somewhat silly and insulted that they are restricted from thinking and speaking broadly about business issues and challenges. But, for the sake of the salary and under peer pressure, they settle in to the limitations of the job. Before long, *they* are the ones telling newcomers to the company, "We just don't do it that way here." A corporate glacier of compliance and complacence ices over even the fieriest minds. The massive weight of that glacier, as felt by each employee, makes the company culture appear to be an immovable object. Contrary ideas or suggestions are buried from the beginning or never offered in the first place by employees who have given up the idea of speaking frankly, clearly, spontaneously, and originally while they are at work.

Scenario 3: Delivering Business Results in the Face of Low Levels of Trust

In this scenario, we follow the trials and tribulations of a well-intentioned, hard-working manager struggling to establish and maintain trust and efficiency among members of several teams separated not only by distance but also by culture, time zones, and work habits. This dilemma is hardly unique. As products and services are increasingly outsourced to cheap labor locations, managers find themselves in the difficult situation of trying to lead and coordinate activities among team members who may never have met, speak different languages, and often fail to see the big picture of how their function fits into the total production plan.

Tom Marshall works for a major technology company with customers and employees in more than thirty countries. Headquartered and founded in Silicon Valley more than twenty years ago, the company has gradually pushed most of its manufacturing, marketing, and customer service units outside of the U.S. The company maintains its headquarters and its technology development and product design operations in California.

Tom has recently been put in charge of overseeing the final stages of manufacturing a new line of servers that operates simultaneously with the three leading operating systems and consumes less energy than a fifty-watt light bulb during a twenty-four-hour period. These new servers are targeted at small to medium businesses with limited in-house IT staff. Tom was put in charge when the original product manager had to take a six-month leave of absence to care for his wife, who is undergoing intensive rehabilitation following an automobile accident. This is a great opportunity for Tom to showcase his engineering and management savvy. He is excited but nervous, as many of his company's products miss their rollout deadlines.

We will follow Tom through the first week of meetings and

conversations as he guides his far-flung project teams toward the finish line. Most of the servers' components are made in the Asian countries of Malaysia, Taiwan, and South Korea. The servers will be assembled and tested in Ireland, with initial product introductions in the U.S. and Europe.

We begin with a meeting between Tom and his manager, the executive vice president for the global business unit that handles all manufacturing and related logistics. Tom's boss lays out the primary challenge of making sure that all components are manufactured according to specifications, quality checked, and delivered to the assembly plant in Ireland in six weeks. The assembly plant then has two weeks to assemble and ship the first one thousand units. This timeline will enable the company to publicly launch the new servers before the close of the third quarter, which looks like it otherwise will be full of mostly disappointing news for investors.

Tom asks a few questions about the major players he will be depending upon to make the tight deadline. Tom's boss is not the kind of guy who puts up with a lot of questions. He is very results oriented and expects his people to be results oriented. He does not answer most of Tom's questions about the project and the personalities and track records of the major players, instead instructing Tom to ask them himself or telling him that he will figure that out soon enough. Tom's boss ends the conversation by relating how important this assignment is to the CEO, and how he knows Tom can "pull this rabbit out of the hat." Over the years, Tom has gotten used to his boss's knack for providing little helpful advice and information for big assignments. He walks out of his meeting more unsettled than usual due to the importance of the project for the company's upcoming quarterly numbers.

The next day, Tom convenes a meeting via videoconference with the project team, the heads of manufacturing of the key components of the new server line. The call includes Tim Pearson in Taipei, Taiwan; Ishak Malanjum in Kuala Lumpur,

Malaysia; Lee Hong-soo in Seoul, South Korea; and Brian Walsh, head of the assembly plant outside of Dublin, Ireland. Tom must align differing personalities, cultures, and priorities in securing buy-in and commitment to the new timeline. He immediately develops serious reservations about the ability of these men to deliver their components quality certified and on time. They seem to take perverse pleasure in Tom being in the hot seat for completing the high visibility server project. He finds little trust among the project team, whose members indirectly criticize one another on several occasions. He is particularly concerned about how well Ishak and Tim will coordinate their efforts since their components must be quality checked together. Each manufacturing head agrees to submit a three-week work plan to Tom within twenty-four hours. Tom asks them several times and in several ways to warn him as soon as any hint of a possible delay occurs. All acknowledge the importance of the project to the company's bottom line and pledge full cooperation. All agree to daily e-mail updates for Tom for the duration of the project.

Two days later, Tom leads a presentation on the server project to the company's executive team, whose members include the CEO, CFO, heads of the major business units, and the head of Human Resources. Executive team members pepper Tom with questions during his presentation. The CFO openly doubts that Tom, or anyone for that matter, can make the launch deadline for the servers. The head of the global sales organization explains that his sales teams have been priming the pump on the new line of servers and reminds Tom about the quality issues still haunting the company's last launch of new servers. Tom remains responsive, professional, and cool as the discussion ranges from the aggressive, take-no-prisoners urgings of the CEO to the "we still do not have enough information to know what's going on here" questioning from other executive team members. He leaves the meeting feeling he has little support if problems arise. No member of the executive team uttered anything close to "Don't hesitate to contact me if you need any help." In fact, the clear message to Tom was: "Don't screw this up. It's too important."

Later that same day, Tom has a telephone conversation with Brian Walsh, head of the assembly plant outside of Dublin. Tom cannot tell if Walsh can actually deliver on his promise to keep the assembly plant running 24/7 to meet the project timeline. Walsh's anticipation of late component deliveries from Malaysia and Taiwan deeply troubles Tom. He does not know if Walsh is giving him a hard time, preemptively setting up an excuse for the Irish assembly plant, or does not grasp the gravity of this project to the company's quarterly results. Walsh ends the call by telling Tom to get to Taipei and Kuala Lumpur right away.

In Tom's last major meeting of the week, he personally briefs the CEO on the challenges and obstacles he has found so far. Tom's boss is present and does not say anything during the entire meeting. The CEO tears into Tom for not getting on top of this project earlier and for not getting on a plane to personally stand over the heads of manufacturing in Taiwan and Malaysia. Tom tries to present a balanced and accurate picture of the project with clear identification of the project's critical paths and potential weaknesses in the project plan and project team. Tom defers from making the commitments or conclusions sought by the demanding CEO. The next day, Tom flies to Taipei.

In these meetings, we see Tom attempting to quickly get on top of an extremely important project. His boss and the CEO do little more than increase the pressure on Tom to deliver. Though he is very dependent on the candor of his project team, it is clear to Tom that his team—Tim Pearson in Taipei, Ishak Malanjum in Kuala Lumpur, Lee Hong-soo in Seoul, and Brian Walsh in Dublin—do not trust one another to meet the project's deliverables to get the first servers shipped in six weeks.

On the plane ride to Taipei, Tom makes the following decisions:

- To personally meet once a week with Tim Pearson in Taipei, Ishak Malanjum in Kuala Lumpur, and Lee Hong-soo in Seoul. While the team members may not have much trust in common, Tom decides that he needs to build trust individually with each. He needs the highest levels of candor possible from each manufacturing head so that if anything starts slipping, he can immediately throw additional resources at the problem area. Tom also wants to build bridges to the management team and line workers at the different manufacturing plants. He wants to put a human face on this project and take it out of being the latest crisis invented by headquarters in California.
- To keep the manufacturing heads talking in twice-a-week videoconference meetings. While he may not be able to rebuild their bonds of trust, he must keep accurate information flowing among these critical players. He has to stay on top of what's working and what's not working as the project team proceeds down its critical path. Tom knows he will need to make mid-course adjustments to meet the tight delivery date.
- To make each manufacturing head designate and use a full-time project lead. These project leads must participate in every meeting of the project team as well as send Tom daily e-mail progress reports. Tom is looking for a way to work around the quibbling of the manufacturing heads. This gives Tom another major point of contact within each manufacturing plant and another person to build trust with in case the heads of manufacturing do not disclose emerging problems.
- To submit weekly one-page progress reports to the executive team. He will personally call each member of the executive team at least once a week to check in and secure buy-in on the project. He hopes this

will result in at least one or two executive team members' help in managing the expectations of the company's leaders and in providing additional resources if necessary.
- To call his boss at least twice a week and copy him on the executive team weekly progress reports. Tom expects nothing from his boss and just wants to keep him off his back.

Tom determines that to meet his deadline and ensure that the servers are delivered, he must work around the low levels of trust within his project team. Distance and the differing cultures of the team leaders in Europe and Asia, combined with trust relationships never established or damaged over time, challenge Tom's ability to move the project forward. In working toward his goal, Tom faces three dilemmas.

Tom quickly identifies the low levels of trust among the leaders of his project team, but how can he build trust individually with each team leader? Should he give up so quickly on establishing higher levels of trust among his team leaders? How can he secure candor from the team leaders in their meetings, reports, and briefings?

Tom's boss and the company's executive team consistently put pressure on Tom but provide little support or assistance. Should Tom spend time on developing an ally within the executive team? Should Tom be open with these executives about the existing low levels of trust within his project team or just focus on the major deliverables of the project in his communications?

Will Tom's effort to put a human face on the project at each of the key locations backfire? Will he undercut the authority of local management? Does he even have enough time to build any kind of trust relationship with local management or workers?

Tom's complicated management dilemma demonstrates how trust and cooperation among team members depends on the degree to which they receive a steady flow of accurate, timely information. Tom recognizes (we hope not too late) that his leadership of an international team requires him to be a "communication architect"—that is, a manager who establishes, monitors, and adjusts a complex web of communication links among his team members. Lacking adequate communication about their goals and deadlines, team members will tend to idle in neutral, awaiting specific instructions, or wing it by trying to perform their jobs based on a very limited understanding of what they should be doing. In either case, trust among team members as well as trust between Tom and the team will suffer. Accused of not meeting project specifications, team members in one country will no doubt react defensively, protesting that they were not told exactly what was wanted or required. As progress on the project goes from bad to worse, blame will be passed around freely by top management, further alienating and discouraging team members and their leader, Tom.

The key point in this short case is the importance of accurate, timely information as a foundation for trust among international teams who may share little else with one another in terms of past work experience, performance expectations, and management culture. Any manager who wants to lead and coordinate a series of connected but semi-independent international work groups is responsible, above all, for a system of communication that will keep all team members informed of one another's activities, project progress, and unexpected workflow interruptions or emergencies.

Chapter Seven

Building Individual Trust in the Workplace

"Every kind of peaceful cooperation among men is primarily based on mutual trust . . ."
                                                    Albert Einstein

Let's say at this point that you accept the importance of trust for business relationships, productivity, loyalty, innovation, and many other must-have attributes of successful organizations and individuals. Moreover, let's assume that you are not satisfied with the level of trust in your own work situation or in your company and that you want to do something about the problem. Where can you start?

The Small Scale: Individual Action to Rebuild Trust

If you choose to begin the path back to workplace trust by changing your own business habits, you can take at least four steps right away (as in, today):

1. Rebuild the basis of trust by shoring up its foundations of candor, assertiveness, and cohesion.

Rediscover how easy and freeing it can be to speak and act with candor, even about the most trivial details of business life. Fear of consequences may have kept you from being candid in small and large matters at work. That fear tends to melt away quickly once you commit yourself to honest statements that do not require later hedging or prevaricating. The consequences that flow from candor are almost always positive. Coworkers, bosses, and subordinates feel respected rather than conned. They are much more likely to respond to your candor in kind. Perhaps they too have felt the complications that emerge when a lack of candor turns work life into a web of mistrust ("What did I tell him and what do I need to say now to keep my story from falling apart?"). In those cases where your candor brings apparent negative responses such as disappointment and anger from others, you can assure yourself that at least you got the problem out on the table where realistic solutions can be discussed. For example, let's say that you have been less than candid about progress on a major report, having told your boss, "It's almost done. We had a network problem that slowed us down." Plain candor—"I need another three days to complete the report"—may arouse impatience and irritation on the part of the boss, but he or she would certainly prefer to know the real state of affairs rather than the fantasy version of "almost done." When the real facts are on the table, the boss is in a position to provide additional support or clear other duties from your calendar to help you complete the report. What's more, this honest confrontation with your boss may inaugurate a new, healthier relationship between the two of you. The boss may become more willing to depend on you for important tasks, knowing that you won't blow smoke about how things are actually going on your projects.

Practicing a lack of candor requires an elaborate set of mental gymnastics wherein one estimates the gullibility of others, strains one's own creative energies to come up with likely stories, and builds a safety net of deniability so as not to get caught. Stop! Take yourself back to that refreshing spontaneity you may have experienced on the first day of your job, a time when you asked questions freely without a scheme in mind, when you gave feedback that reflected what you actually thought rather than what others wanted you to say, when you felt your job was to tell it like it is. A return to candor does not guarantee that you will always be right in what you say; no one has that track record. But candor does demonstrate influentially to others that you speak your mind and that you are a so-called straight shooter. Candor tears down the fear of consequences as you find yourself speaking and acting naturally and often courageously in circumstances that tempt others to hide or distort what they think and feel. Talking to a person who lacks candor is like trying to see someone through a dirty window: the obscuring barrier of glass is all you can focus on. By contrast, speaking to a candid person is like seeing a person through a spotless pane of glass, so transparent that it seems not to be there. Candor says, in effect, "I'm not putting any barriers, stratagems, affectations, phoniness, or game playing between us. What you see is who I am."

Otherwise honest, candid people sometimes slip back down the slope toward a lack of candor by what they don't say rather than by what they do say. They sit at meetings and remain silent while objectionable plans and ideas move forward toward implementation. They play it safe through silence or noncommittal comments in interviews, meetings, and other forums where their opinions could make a difference. Here is where assertiveness leads you back to trust. Being assertive does not require that you become aggressive. It does mean that you value your own insights and recognize that by withholding them, you may be avoiding your responsibility to your company and to yourself. A good test of assertiveness is to monitor how often (and how well) you contribute your opinions, perspectives, and ideas during meetings with your work group. If you decide that you sit back as a passive spectator while others do battle in the arena of company action, it's time to reenter the fray. By asserting your insights, of course, you do not guarantee that group decisions and votes will go your way. But the opposite is certainly true: if others don't know what you think, there is no chance that your ideas will become part of the mix that leads to decisions and action.

We can all imagine a person who is candid and assertive but fails to be effective in the workplace because he or she is a "lone wolf," unwilling to involve others or consider their positions, in other words, not a cohesive part of the group. Working toward cohesion is an abbreviated way of describing a cluster of desirable qualities:

- Being open to the ideas of others without losing touch with one's own perspectives
- Taking time to build relationships with others that allow ideas to flow easily from person to person without interruptive suspicions about ulterior motives
- Sharing credit where credit is due with others who contributed time, insight, and energy to a task or project
- Giving feedback to others so they know where they stand in relation to you and your priorities, insights, and goals
- Supporting others, especially coworkers who need your specific expertise or experience in completing their work.

Increasingly, major scientific, cultural, and civic awards such as the Nobel Prize and the various Pulitzer Prizes are awarded to teams rather than to individuals. Even when a physicist, biologist, or political leader is singled out for recognition, these individuals inevitably pay tribute in their acceptance speeches to the team, the support of an organization, or their fellow researchers. What's true of Nobel winners, in terms of their involvement in team cohesion, should be no less true of us as we take proactive steps to restore trust—or bring it aboard for the first time.

2. Recognize and show appreciation for the building blocks of trust observed in others.

It is commonplace to remark that we don't thank one another often enough in business life. If we do say thanks, it is usually not much more than a perfunctory, end-of-conversation bookend that lets the other person know we will be walking away. Here are three mini-scenarios in which an expression of gratitude takes on an important role in encouraging trust behavior.

In the first example, assume one of your subordinates knocks on your office door. She is obviously upset. "Sue, what's the matter?" you inquire. She visibly summons her courage and says, "I know it's your right to give my assistant any tasks you want to—you're the boss. But it would really help me manage my unit better if you came through me whenever possible so I can keep the whole work schedule. What happened this morning is that she did your job right away, but didn't do a job I had given her, one that had to go out by FedEx today. She was afraid of disappointing you."

What are your options? You could react temperamentally to Sue, telling her, "You're right I'm the boss, and that means my priorities are *the* priorities around here!" Sue would probably not say another word at the time, but the negative result of your confrontation with her would be played out for months or years in how she did her job.

On the other hand, you might recognize that Sue intended no insubordination or lack of respect for you. She trusted that giving her opinion on how work can best be accomplished in the work unit would not upset you. You can choose to respond to the content of her message by saying, "You're right. I'll check with you next time." But if you want to encourage trust, you would also validate Sue's willingness to bring an awkward issue to your attention: "Sue, I'm glad you felt that you could talk to me about this. It takes some moxie and trust to call your boss on a work problem. Thanks for the trust you showed in talking to me. And you're absolutely right; I don't want to interfere with your work flow by grabbing people off tasks you've assigned them to. I'll check with you next time I have a rush job and we'll coordinate, okay?" Sue walks back to her office encouraged by the trust bond that has been strengthened between the two of you. Dividends get paid in her motivation to give her best effort to you and her job.

In another scenario, you sit in one of the final meetings in your division before the marketing launch of a new software product that allows personal computers to show HDTV programs. The VP of Marketing has indicated (in a twenty-minute harangue to meeting attendees) that the vast majority of advertising will be directed to the eighteen and under market. Because the VP is a bull of a man both in stature and personality, and because he seems to have the ear of the CEO (who is sitting just to his left), no one crosses him at meetings. As he winds up his speech, you notice a quizzical or frustrated look on many faces in the room. Yet when the VP opens the floor to questions, no one has a word to say. Silence is taken as assent; the VP says, in fact, "I'm pleased you have no objections and I'll take your lack of questions to mean that you're ready to move ahead with the marketing plan I've described."

You can't help yourself. You raise your hand just a bit to catch his attention and begin to speak your piece: "Based on my limited knowledge of network sports programs, virtually all big sporting events from baseball to football to ice-skating will be broadcast this year in HD. These events typically draw an older audience, but a large audience. I'm wondering if we're missing a lot of potential sales by limiting our marketing efforts to the eighteen and under group." The VP huffs and puffs, obviously irritated by having his judgment and his plan questioned. He refers with a wave of his hand to "many demographic studies" and "expert media consultants."

When the meeting is over, the CEO approaches you. You've had only a few one-on-one contacts with her; you worry that you are about to be told you're unemployed. To your surprise, the CEO says, "I just wanted you to know that I appreciated your question about the direction of the marketing campaign. It took a lot of guts to swim against the tide. I'm glad you feel like this is the kind of company where you can raise objections, even to very popular policies and programs. Keep up the good work." You mumble a few words of thanks, then head to your office. In your seven years with the company, your work has been praised many times by executives. But not one of them ever expressed appreciation for your occasional role as the "loyal opposition." You feel good about the compliment and resolve to speak your mind more often in the company when you see people and programs headed in what you feel are the wrong direction.

In our last case, you've been with the company for four years and recently received your promotion to manager. As such, you head up a group of fourteen people. You believe that their participation in decision making is crucial to morale and productivity, so you schedule an all-hands meeting on the first and third Monday mornings of each month. You have had two meetings so far and you have your doubts whether to ever have another. The meetings to date have been just plain awful. You end up doing 90 percent of the talking because no one else will offer ideas, opinions, perspectives, or even objections. The meeting attendees just sit there, often looking at their hands or the floor. When you pose a direct question to the group, no one speaks up. In desperation, you've taken to calling on particular people: "John, what do you think about the proposed benefits package?" John makes no eye contact and seems to be terribly uncomfortable being "picked on" so publicly. "I dunno," he mumbles. "Okay by me, I guess." That kind of response wasn't what you had in mind by "participation." Determined to find out why your meetings are going so sour, you catch two of your more communicative employees during a coffee break. "I'm sure you don't want to listen to me talk for ninety minutes straight," you tell them. "But what else can I do? No one wants to discuss anything. Why don't people speak up?" The answers don't come quickly from the two employees, but eventually they do surface. "Our old manager had a nasty habit of telling his boss exactly what each of us said in our meetings," one employee reveals. "In fact, some bits of conversation we thought were private to our meeting showed up in our performance evaluations. That put the big chill on everyone's willingness to volunteer ideas and opinions. None of us trusted the old manager and I guess you've inherited some of those attitudes."

At your next meeting, you set about repairing the substantial damage to trust done by the former manager. Your first act is to send the recording secretary out of the room with the explanation that the two of you will figure out the minutes after the meeting: "No one is taking specifics notes on what any of us have to say." You then explain why you want people to speak up with their comments and ideas—"not because I want to catch you in some kind of trap," you say, "and certainly not because I'm going to pass along what you say to my boss. I consider the doors to our meeting closed for a reason. We have to feel comfortable speaking openly and freely with one another. You each have information and observations that I need to know and the company needs to know. That information isn't going to come out if I do all the talking in our meetings." To your gratification, quiet voices grow louder little by little until by the fourth or fifth meeting, all attendees are happily contributing valuable comments and questions. With the rise in meeting participation comes a parallel rise in group productivity. The trust that had been broken by a former manager was gradually rebuilt.

Catching your employees doing something right and recognizing them for it, even by a simple expression of thanks, can encourage those desired behaviors in the future. Especially when a subordinate wonders whether to offer an opinion contrary to that of the boss, your words of encouragement and appreciation to that subordinate can play a key role in building the person's confidence in his or her own judgments. Trust among workers and managers grows as frank discussion becomes the expected norm in the company rather than a high-risk behavior.

3. Model trustworthy behavior and communication as a way of locating supportive coworkers.

Frank Serpico, as portrayed in director Sidney Lumet's 1973 movie titled *Serpico*, was a real-life New York cop who blew the whistle on widespread police corruption only to have his fellow officers turn against him. Few of us have the staying power to be a lone Serpico figure in an organization that does not value trust, including its building blocks in the form of candor, assertiveness, and cohesion. There's the ever-present danger that, over time, we will give up our own commitments and values simply out of exhaustion after bumping heads with distrustful people in the company. The bottom line, we may decide, is that trust involves "two hands clapping," a partnership between trusting and trustworthy individuals. Finding even a few such people in your work environment can give you the intestinal fortitude and moral courage to press on with personal candor and the rest in the face of surrounding deceptions and fabrications. A 2007 management study by Dr. Michael Phelps at the University of Washington determined that bad apples in the workplace do corrupt the bunch but also that their corrosive influence can be overcome by even a few individuals committed to candor and trust. Unlike actual apples in a basket, the good apples (so to speak) in the workplace can exert a salutary effect on the bad, turning around their behavior, attitudes, and influence. Unlike Frank Serpico, who found no trustworthy partner with whom to share his personal opposition to police corruption, an individual intent on rebuilding trust at work needs to locate other points of light with whom he or she can speak candidly. Trust is always a team sport. No one plays it alone.

Here's the experience of a work group in the government grants division of a large biotech company. The group manager, Brent, knew he had a trust problem on his hands. Every meeting told him so, as his employees played it safe by waiting for someone else to speak and hoping that Brent would not call on them directly by name. Brent also knew the reasons for this distrust. Six months prior the company had announced a layoff of 15 percent of workers but claimed that natural attrition would account for these laid-off employees. No one who wanted to stay on the payroll, the company said, would be let go. In the intervening months, that company promise had proven worthless. In Brent's group alone, eight long-term employees had received their lay-off notices and were now gone, with little hope of returning. The legacy of the company's mishandling of layoffs now could be observed every day in the inconsistent performance by the remaining employees. They took sick days whenever possible, arrived late to work and left early, and generally kept to themselves during the work day, except for frantic gossip sessions that made up the lunch hour. Brent understood their frustration but also had a group to run—for his own sake, in terms of his career, as well as for the company's sake.

Brent knew that he couldn't simply make a "rah-rah" speech about trust and teamwork. His workers still had a bitter taste in their mouths for those sentiments. He decided, instead, simply to practice trust with one individual, then two, hoping to build his circle of positive influence outward to eventually incorporate the entire crew. He started by having short daily conversations with Evelyn, an older worker who had seen both the good times and the bad times in the company. "Evelyn," he said in one of these conversations, "I have a problem. I need to talk to someone about a work issue, but it's not the kind of thing I want to take to my boss. Do you have a moment?" Evelyn at that instant felt simultaneously complimented and perplexed: complimented that the boss would single her out for a confidential conversation, but also perplexed by what he wanted from her. Did he expect her to keep a secret of some kind? Was she in some kind of trouble?

Brent went on to discuss the trust problem with Evelyn: "I realize you all feel burned by what the company did. You saw a lot of longtime friends lose their jobs, and no doubt you worry about losing your own. I can't change what the company did. But living under that dark cloud in our own work group isn't good for any of us. Someone has to start trusting someone around here. And I want to build that trust with each of my people, no matter how long it takes. Take this conversation, for example. I want to earn your trust that I'm not setting you up for any surprises or manipulating you to be a messenger of any kind to other employees. I just want your trust. It's that simple. I'll be candid and open with you about developments in the company and answer your questions to the best of my ability."

Evelyn broke in: "That's really all people have been asking for around here. We feel that we're the last ones to find out information that affects our jobs and lives. And that's after twenty years with the company for some of us!"

Brent replied, "I get it and I know the company has some apologizing to do. But until that happens, I want our work group to get back onto an even keel where we at least trust one another even if we can't say the same for the whole company."

"I couldn't agree more, but how do you see that happening?" Evelyn asked.

Brent answered, "Pretty much like this: regular conversations where we talk about what we're facing on the job and how we can work together more productively and enjoyably. I don't think anyone is having much fun at work these days."

Evelyn responded, "No joke. It feels like a morgue."

Brent laughed. "So here's my idea. Starting with you and me, we're going to start a first-thing-in-the-morning get-together for anyone who wants to attend, a coffee klatch where we all put aside our titles and just talk frankly about what we're thinking and feeling at work, and how we can turn things around to our own advantage."

Evelyn agreed. "Let's give it a try."

Within a month, all of Brent's employees were showing up (on time) first thing in the morning so that the group had to take over a section of the cafeteria for the weekly get-together. Topics ranged widely from company policies to rumors about the competition to priorities for training classes. Everyone spoke up. Brent could see friendships, bruised by the layoffs, start to bloom again. Communication with individual employees became vastly easier for Brent. He could speak his mind without having to filter his messages to others through their screens of attitude and apprehension. And much more communication came *from* employees these days. In a word, they had learned to trust their boss.

4. Measure and evaluate your own trust level within the workplace.

It's one thing to look across the office and make judgments about Fred, Alice, and Juan with regard to their trustworthiness. It's quite another task, and a more difficult one, to "see ourselves as others see us," in the words of Robert Burns. Gauging your own level of trust involves two dimensions: To what degree do I trust others at work? And, to what degree do others trust me?

The Employee to Employee Survey in Chapter Ten is a good place to begin. Once you have marked the test as candidly as possible (hedging on a test that measures trust gets us nowhere!), review your results, preferably with a friend with whom you can discuss issues and answers. You may find that you exhibit high levels of trust in some relationships, perhaps with your coworkers, and somewhat less so in other relationships, say, that with your boss. In coming to terms with your own level of trust, don't focus exclusively on the less-than-I-would-like categories. Instead, think through the forces and circumstances that make it natural and easy for you to be trustworthy in your high-scoring categories. Then, with those insights in mind, turn to your lower-scoring categories. What is it about those circumstances, personalities, or relationships that makes it more difficult to act in a wholly trustworthy way? It's a good idea to jot down your reflections and conclusions in a personal journal. Often we spend more time keeping written track of the mileage and service record for our car than we do for our own thoughts and feelings having to do with work.

Also think about trust from the other direction, perhaps using data provided by the instruments in Chapter Ten: Do people trust me, and to what extent?

Chapter Eight

Trust for the New Workforce

"Few things help an individual more than to place responsibility upon him, and to let him know that you trust him."
Booker T. Washington

This chapter visits a crucial issue for virtually all employers: How can I build high-trust relationships with the new generation of employees, those who seem to have such different lifestyles and habits compared to the rest of the older workforce? "They looked human," one senior manager complained of his youngest employees, "but they didn't act or sound that way. They were into Facebook and MySpace and computer games I had never heard of. They talked about YouTube videos instead of books or the news. I didn't understand them. I didn't know if I could trust them to be responsible on big projects or with clients. Worst of all, I never had the feeling they trusted me. I've never felt so old in my life as when I'm around them. And I'm only forty-seven!"

How can a manager learn to trust his or her Millennial workers? How can a manager earn their trust in return? To address those questions, let's first get to know the young men and women we're discussing.

The term "Millennial" denotes a person born between 1982 and 2000—the mid- and late-life children of the baby boom generation (born 1945 through 1965) and the children of the Generation Xers. William Strauss and Neil Howe coined the term in their popular book, *Millennials Rising*. Millennials are often the last child ("baby of the family") or only child of boomers, and as such have enjoyed a somewhat coddled upbringing. However, upbringing alone doesn't account for Millennial behavior. Media influences, social networking, and the changing norms of society have much more to do with it. These are young people who, in general, have:

- Competed for good grades in rigorous school environments. High school and college were not "easy" for Millennials.
- Confronted standardized tests (SSAT, ACT, SAT) as the primary gateway to the colleges of their choice. Millennials didn't get by on a smile for the teacher.
- Established dozens—often hundreds—of chatty acquaintances in cyberspace (Facebook, MySpace) rather than a handful of in-depth, in-person friendships.
- Relied on their parents as life coaches, financiers, travel organizers, tutors, ghost writers, and advocates vis-à-vis authority figures such as principals and employers.
- Lived at home without responsibilities.
- Used alcohol and, to a lesser extent, drugs as a means of social bonding ("the party scene").
- Accepted casual sex ("hookups") without negative moral judgments but with relatively firm attitudes about personal respect and sexual protection.
- Avoided long-term monogamous relationships, including early marriage.
- Had access to enough money for "in" clothing, music, cars (their own or their parents'), vacation travel, and the sporting life (skiing, surfing, biking).
- Believed his baby boomer parents settled for the dehumanizing aspects of the workplace to secure financial independence.
- Valued a slim, fit, groomed appearance.

- Participated in competitive sports without self-consciousness or anxiety over being labeled a "jock."
- Used music as their constant ambient environment while studying, driving, relaxing, and working.
- Looked upon their managers and supervisors as surrogate parents—adults with whom they are eager to have a one-on-one relationship without concern about hierarchy or organizational power.
- Viewed their jobs as relatively short term in duration (like a summer job)—one that they can quit at any time without stigma from parents, friends, or coworkers if they become bored, experience problems with coworkers or bosses, or are attracted to more interesting work elsewhere.
- Embraced 24/7 electronic connections with their extended social network through computers, cell phones, iPods, and other devices.
- Bypassed traditional political affiliation and religious membership for a more diffuse set of social attitudes and involvements centered on protecting the environment, helping the poor, and eliminating discrimination.

In the previous list, certainly the experiences of Millennials overlap in many instances with similar life experiences for boomers and Generation Xers. In fact, in locating these areas of common experiences, separate generations can often find the basis for engendering trust both in and out of professional life.

Millennials, Trust, and Authority Figures

It would not be atypical for a baby boomer taking a new job to meet the boss with obvious signs of deference: nervous smiles, ready expressions of agreement, a concern for not taking up too much of the boss's time, and above all a fear of breaking work rules or social conventions. The baby boomer may trust the boss to be fair—that is, abide by the rules at work—but probably finds it more difficult to think of or trust the boss as a friend. Once the baby boomer is hired and shown to a desk, he or she works there from eight or nine to five. The baby boomer employee does not often confront or question company decisions. This worker does not regularly communicate that he or she has better ideas than the boss. Trust has its limits. Innovative suggestions, if given at all, have to be requested by the boss as a work order of sorts. These suggestions are then offered tentatively, humbly, and often in watered-down form, lest the boss find offense in "upstart" behavior on the part of the employee.

By contrast, the Millennial meets the boss much as he met his girlfriend's parents—a friendly handshake, a genuine smile, and talk, talk, talk. The Millennial is eager to get beyond formalities and discover what the boss is "into." Unless told to use a surname, the Millennial is likely to call the boss by his or her first name. Far from sitting at a desk from eight to five, this worker roves around the office, finding out what others are doing, chatting about whatever comes to mind, obeying no boundary between at-work and after-work conversations, and getting help with tasks from whomever is willing. The Millennial is highly aware of the role of personality in the workplace and works on being liked, being thought "cool" (or its modern-day equivalent), and having many mock-teasing, surface-level social contacts with other workers during the workday. When a Millennial says "it's a great job," he or she is probably referring not to the actual work or compensation but rather to the banter, play, and fun that characterizes the work environment.

Does the Millennial trust the boss? Yes and no. The freedom with which the Millennial engages his or her supervisor certainly suggests a form of trust. Who would be so casual and disclosing with someone they didn't trust? On the other hand, baby boomer bosses quickly sense that they are not "part of the club" when they are in the presence of Millennials. The boss doesn't keep up with people through Facebook or MySpace.

Blogs aren't his way to get or give information. The boss does surf the Web for news and information, but also still reads the newspaper—imagine! It's just that his ways are different from the Millennial ways of getting things done. His approach seems so plodding. In short, Millennials can't trust him to get with the program.

The Millennial sees no reason not to tell the boss what he or she thinks on any particular topic, whether related to work or not. For the boss not to listen with sincere interest to the Millennial's ideas and opinions would be viewed by the Millennial as "the boss's problem," not as the new worker's violation of workplace hierarchies and conventions. If the boss gives a Millennial a tedious task below his or her abilities, the Millennial is apt to speak up not so much to object to the lowbrow work as to remind the boss that talent is being wasted. The Millennial enjoys working with a highly socialized team and does not mind sharing credit for accomplishments. "Getting ahead," to the Millennial, more often means being assigned to increasingly interesting or challenging projects than being in charge of increasing numbers of his or her peers or getting more money than his friends at work.

Trust and the Social Network

Millennials are in almost constant communication, even during work hours, with many friends and acquaintances. The nature of these communications may seem shallow in the extreme—a quick series of back-and-forth text messages consisting of one- or two-letter words and emoticons [(-:] or a brief instant-message chat focused on what is going on at the moment. In fact, the sum total of such communications with another person proves to be quite complex and layered in the subtlety, sensitivity to feelings, and breadth of topics touched on. Trust is built up quickly by snippets of feeling, disclosure, wit, sentimental response, and caring (though abbreviated) feedback. The conversation doesn't have to be in real time. "Comments" to "posts" on blogs and Facebook or MySpace sites are occasions for wit (or not), venting, sympathy, teasing, and flirting. These light touches, by the dozen during the day and night, provide entrée and stimulus to get-togethers, party invitations, dates, and other social activities.

Successful social networking requires almost nonstop disclosure of personal feelings and experiences. Unlike their more circumspect and private boomer parents, Millennials find it easy to disclose even the most intimate details of their no-longer-private lives to dozens of permitted visitors and thousands of others to their blogs, Facebook, and MySpace sites. On such social networks, a young woman may self-describe herself, without embarrassment or self-consciousness, as "a fox who parties hard." A young man may tell the world he is into "booze, women, and soccer, in that order." Hourly or even minute-by-minute disclosure of this kind at Internet sites breeds a mindset for Millennials that carries over into professional life. They use personal details as primary tools for establishing and maintaining relationships, including work relationships with their bosses and peers. A Millennial is much more likely than a boomer to blurt out to a boss, "Sorry I'm late. I partied late last night" or to tell an all-ears coworker about sexual experiences. Popular TV shows such as *The Office* are based in large part on the awkward and often hilarious tension in the workplace between the disclosing antics of Millennials versus the staid behavior of boomers. The workplace, like Internet social networks, becomes a primary venue for social life for Millennials, presenting new challenges in maintaining a productive and non-hostile work environment.

Millennials use their social network freely to vent and problem solve. For example, if a boss reacts negatively and critically to a Millennial's work, the Millennial will "tell the world" within minutes via his or her blog or Facebook or MySpace site. This social network will then buzz for hours with supportive outrage ("the jerk"), advice ("here's what I would tell him"), and sympathy ("hang in there"). Companies are named freely at such sites as "a terrible place to work" and "business hell." Offending bosses are described in close enough detail so that they are easily identified, if not named outright. In their online disclosures, Millennials act as if their communications will only be seen by their intended network of friends. They express surprise and sometimes outrage when a boss "googles" a Millennial's name, only to discover a steady diatribe of complaints and accusations about the company.

The social network is also a brain trust with good ideas, suggested Internet links, and personal connections, all offered freely to anyone in the circle of friends and acquaintances. These people chime in with employment opportunities, restaurant recommendations, movie reactions, and a host of other items of information and opinion. The old wisdom "It's not what you know, it's who you know" has returned triumphant in the form of social networks.

Maintaining Trust through Constant Communication

Baby boomers collected appliances—washers, driers, toasters, ranges, refrigerators, microwave ovens, TVs (in all sizes), stereos, blenders, juicers, slicers/dicers, and bread machines—to create the sensation of security and achievement for a generation craving a level of comfort and status beyond that enjoyed by their parents. The latest and best appliances constituted a social statement, as demonstrated in the boomer phenomenon of perpetual kitchen, bath, and home remodeling. For boomers, the home itself became public testimony and advertising of its residents' financial success, decorating taste, and class memberships or aspirations.

Millennials, uninterested in competing head-to-head with their parents for collections of appliances and all they symbolize, have opted for an alternate set of expensive possessions, most of them chip-based. According to Reynol Junco and Jeanna Mastrodicasa in their 2007 survey of 7,705 college students,

- 97 percent own a computer
- 94 percent own a cell phone (and use it also for telling time, making wristwatches largely passé for Millennials)
- 76 percent use instant messaging (IM)
- 15 percent of IM users are logged on twenty-four hours a day, seven days a week
- 34 percent use Web sites as their primary source of news
- 28 percent own a blog and 44 percent read blogs
- 49 percent download music using peer-to-peer file sharing
- 75 percent of students fourteen years and older have a Facebook account
- 90 percent of college students have a MySpace account and almost all teenagers over the age of sixteen have one
- 60 percent own some type of expensive portable music and/or video device such as an iPod

Anyone who has worked with Millennials knows that these numbers are exceedingly conservative, with true figures trending steeply upward in almost all categories.

Earlier generations found common ground in shared *content*—novels that "everyone" had read, blockbuster movies seen by all, and the exploits of sports teams and heroes. Millennials focus less on common content and much more on their common ground in *connections*, the array of devices, portals, sites, and other ways to connect. They may not see the same video clips on YouTube, but they all know what YouTube is and how to use it.

Trust in the Future: Waiting for Wealth

Millennials seem to have ready cash or sufficient credit to do pretty much whatever they wish, within limits. Fortunately, the financial demands of an information- and communication-obsessed existence are not overwhelming. Once a computer, cell phone, and iPod have been purchased, the Millennial has few other material needs. He or she lives at home without paying rent. Moreover, Mom and Dad often "help out" with what amounts to an adult allowance while the Millennial is "getting started." Especially in urban settings, Millennials are often proud to do without a car, finding that public transportation suits not only their budgets, but also their social and environmental priorities.

The panic that gripped baby boomers who had only a few hundred dollars to their name does not seem to disturb the calm and confidence of Millennials. Like characters in Dickens' *Great Expectations*, many Millennials begin their careers in the full knowledge that they stand to inherit hundreds of thousands of dollars once their parents have passed away and the family residence is sold (or stocks cashed out, remainder of retirement accounts liquidated, and so forth). A twenty-year-old Millennial with parents in their fifties can calculate with some assurance that his or her own middle age will be financially comfortable based on inherited wealth, not the fruit of his or her own labor. This reality for many Millennials encourages a somewhat whimsical attitude toward work, career, and "making it." Since Millennials generally do not aspire to the same kind of material possessions as their parents (for example, a large house in the suburbs with four children and a dog), they are less driven to pursue huge salaries at the expense of day-to-day lifestyle.

That such wealth is on its way is assured simply by demographics. According to the Census Bureau, one in five Americans will be sixty-five or older by 2030. More than half (54 percent) of present-day employees will leave the workforce in the next decade. By 2012, Millennials will comprise 70 percent of American employees. In this period, their wealth-conscious parents will undoubtedly continue to accumulate capital through appreciation of their cherished real estate and investment assets. Boomers are predisposed to "saving it for the kids" rather than spending their wealth on themselves in their elder years.

Discussing the relation of some Millennials to present or future wealth is not meant to suggest that all Millennials are to the manor born. Far from inheriting wealth, many Millennials find themselves in the difficult position of supporting their elderly parents who either have not saved for retirement or have lived beyond their savings. In some ethnic and regional groups, Millennials commonly work to eat and survive from paycheck to paycheck. Due to high unemployment rates and low educational achievement, these young men and women are seldom those who show up to apply for white collar corporate positions. The impression of the wealthy or about-to-be-wealthy Millennial, therefore, stems more from those on the radar screen of company recruiters than from an accurate averaging of financial status of Millennials across all social groups.

An eighty-hour workweek makes no sense to many Millennials because nothing of personal importance is gained by such a crushing schedule. One's iPod doesn't contain more tunes, one's cell phone doesn't work better, and one's Facebook or MySpace doesn't gain more visitors. If anything, a workaholic regimen inhibits a Millennial's enjoyment of these social and entertainment connections. Although Millennials do not drop out, as hippies did in the 1960s, they certainly opt out of arduous work opportunities that their parents would have seen as difficult but golden opportunities to get ahead.

These crucial differences in the definition of wealth and how it is to be acquired often strain trust between boomers and Generation Xers (perhaps managers in mid- to late-career stages) and the Millennial employees. One form of trust between a manager and an employee centers on the assumption that the manager understands the employee's basic priorities. Traditionally, one such basic priority has been the steady need of the employee for a regular paycheck. Trusting that work motive, the manager can strategize on how to best motivate the employee and find mutually agreed-upon work requirements.

But what happens when a manager must admit, "I just don't get my young employees. They don't seem to care as much about money as my older workers." In this case, a new base of trust must be forged—a new set of assumptions—that allows a manager to plan effectively for workplace productivity. For example, in the case of Millennial workers, a manager may relocate the basis of trust away from traditional motivators such as money and more toward the willingness of Millennials to speak their minds to anyone who takes the time to listen (as opposed to the mantra of the 1960s, "Don't trust anyone over thirty"). In short, the basis of trust depends on the nature and priorities of the individuals involved.

The Breakdown of Trust: Mental Claustrophobia

One of the least remarked but most telling characteristics of Millennials is their impatience with locked-in, linear experiences of any kind. It would prove torturous to most Millennials, for example, to sit through a forty-five-minute training video dealing with the operation and maintenance of a particular company machine. Millennials want to learn the same way they play—mouse always at the ready to click away to another URL, eyes quickly scanning the screen for desired items of information, communication coming at them from a variety of sources (cell phone, instant messaging, text messaging) while they are simultaneously "on task"—with the comforting option that they can, at any moment, change directions or quit entirely. Millennials would predictably rankle at an employee orientation session consisting of "talking heads" at the front of the room. By contrast, these new workers would enjoy discussion tables where they can share personal stories, ask questions, and meet their peers.

It has been charged that Millennials have a short attention span. Nothing could be further from the facts for the generation that spends countless consecutive hours on video games such as *Halo III*. Their parents never focused on anything so long and so single-mindedly. Millennials are impatient with perceptual experiences that deny them control and the ability to select compelling aspects in a nonlinear way. Millennials correctly interpret their sensation of boredom as the incipient death of learning. They respond to boredom by opting out of uninteresting material and attempting to move elsewhere to better stuff. When the nature of the experience (a videotape or film, for example) makes such mental movement and escape impossible, the Millennial is unhappy. He or she acts out feelings of impatience in ways their parents' generation would judge to be ornery and disruptive: chatting with one another instead of "concentrating," checking e-mail or blogs on one's laptop, asking questions and raising issues out of context with the linear material being presented, or just "going to ground" by appearing to zone out.

Millennials' distaste for linear experiences (a training videotape, for example) shows up in their difficulty with business writing. Many Millennials cannot create a cogent, well-supported argument in a memo or report, but not because they are uneducated or dense. Millennials inhabit an intellectual world where discrete thoughts float separate and disjoined from one another, like individual bubble-questions on an SAT test. Millennials resist connecting ideas to one another in a traditional structure of sustained thought much in the same way that they resist linear lectures, tapes, and films. These new workers are more adept at seeing why ideas don't hang together than in forging outlines and arguments. They are superb troubleshooters but ironically can't draw a target to save their professional lives.

The trust gap here for managers lies in the inability or unwillingness of older managers to count on Millennials to carry through a traditional business activity—viewing a training video, for example, or creating a cogent PowerPoint presentation—without constant supervision and prodding. To repair this trust gap, older managers can recognize that Millennials resist some functions of business that were commonplace and expected in former days. These managers can then reconceptualize work activities so that they are more in harmony with the perceptual habits and preferences of their younger workers. Millennials, on the other hand, can be made aware that what they prefer, in terms of job duties and daily activities, may not be what the organization needs. The work world does not have to always or automatically bend to the wishes of its newest workers. Once those workers understand that the older manager's way of doing things has a purpose, Millennials are capable of moving away from their preferences and opt instead for a work style compromise in which both the older manager's and the younger workers' needs are accommodated. This kind of compromise, forged through open discussion of the issues and a bit of experimentation, can restore workplace trust, the ability to rely on one another.

Building a Global Sense of Trust through Causes and Commitments

Millennials are widely committed to social and environmental causes, surprisingly so, given the gaps in social conscience they experienced while growing up in the materialistic nests of their boomer parents. Interestingly, Millennials have not turned college campuses into battlegrounds of protest, as occurred in the 1960s, nor have they poured much energy into the traditional political system. The number of Millennials who go to the polls to vote is the lowest of any age grouping, with senior citizens being the highest.

This is to say that Millennials are far from strategic in their exercise of group power for ethical, environmental, or social improvement. Like their social connections on Facebook and MySpace, allegiances and loyalties to causes such as "green" businesses and alternative energy sources seem to be deeply tinged with the social value and peer popularity of those causes. It pays social dividends on the open stage of cyberspace to present oneself as caring, sensitive, and committed to general principles and projects that one's peers are also occupied with. Facebook and MySpace are usually not venues for the expression of highly individualistic politics or contrarian social attitudes. Such a display would threaten a Millennial's chances of building a large and approving social network. Rebels who aren't funny don't fare well in social networking; Che and Fidel would not have found this connection particularly useful.

Trust, above all, is a shared belief among individuals that they can count on one another to act on the basis of certain assumptions. As they enter the business world, Millennials look to one another to discover what they have in common, what they can count on one another to think, feel, and do in specific business situations. For example, Millennials generally trust one another to lobby for "green" causes and adaptations within business organizations. Millennials trust one another to put talent ahead of seniority as the basis of promotions and company rewards. These kinds of trust bonds, based on age and common experiences, extend beyond any one region or country. It is likely that Millennial high-tech workers in major trading nations such as the U.S., Japan, Korea, and India share more (in other words, trust one another more) in their basic assumptions about work life than they do vis-à-vis their own parents.

Putting Trust to the Test: Challenging the System

If Millennials are quite selective in how they go about "thinking globally," they are fearless when it comes to "thinking locally" about how to improve systems, give the boss advice, make their day more enjoyable, and "work smart." Baby boomers, particularly in large, slow moving, bureaucratic organizations quickly learned to accept a high degree of inefficiency, even stupidity, as "the way things are done around here." Millennials, by and large, feel that it is just plain wrong to do something repeatedly in a way that makes no sense, even if one is being paid well to do so. Millennials are constantly on the Internet prowl for technical fixes, software improvements, and operational shortcuts that satisfy the needs of their intelligence for a rational, better-ordered work world. In the same way that Millennials become apoplectic over a wrong software application at work, they often react just as strongly to arbitrary personnel actions, including inaccurate performance evaluations. Millennials want to know how you got to that conclusion and will tend to badger a superior if they feel that a personnel process is logically flawed.

Mom and Dad may have accepted the raw exercise of power in organizations as the way of the world, but Millennials see no reason to stand by when they perceive an injustice at work. More than any previous generation, they have the option to vote with their feet by quitting their jobs. Many employers are finding this phenomenon to be the single largest detractor when it comes to hiring and training Millennial employees. Backed by parental wealth and unencumbered by fears of social shame due to unemployment, Millennials don't have a high threshold for administrative irritation at work. Millennials can prove to be exceedingly expensive employees not so much because of the salaries they require but because of their penchant for quitting at the first flutter of ruffled feathers at work.

Managing Trust to Manage Millennials

Consider each of the following eight mini-cases involving the management of Millennial workers. Before reading on to one (but not the only) suggested solution, ask yourself how trust can play a key role in increasing the work satisfaction and productivity of these young employees.

Situation 1: You have several Millennials in your office who seem to be playing as much as working during the business day. What do you do to keep them more focused on work?

Millennials are probably convinced that you do not understand what makes them tick, nor are you aware of their need for frequent interpersonal contact, bursts of silliness, and bouts of teasing, sarcastic banter during the workday. It wasn't like this in your father's office, you tell yourself, but you are now (in their eyes) the grandfather. Consider having a "trust conference" at an all-hands employee meeting. Explain your goals for getting work done well in the office, but also indicate your willingness to let your employees have a hand in designing the work environment and social norms for work life (much as Apple employees opted for casual dress that contrasted markedly from the IBM blue-suiters). Your purpose is to trust your Millennial workers to be self-monitoring in the balance they strike between playing hard and working hard.

Situation 2: One of your Millennials comes to you to say that she has a chance to go to Ireland for the summer with friends. She wants your okay to miss work for three months without pay. You have a heavy workload coming up for the summer and had counted on her as one of your team to get the work done. How do you respond to her request, assuming you don't want to lose her as an employee?

Millennials typically don't understand why you can't make exceptions. Their parents did. Their teachers did. Their friends do. It's unlikely, therefore, that you will find an understanding ear for the position that, "Well, if I let you take time off, I'll have to let everyone do so." Therefore, decide in advance if you can afford to have this employee take three months off without pay.

Once that decision is made, communicate the decision to her as a matter of trust and need: "I really need you this summer. The work just won't get done without you. I count on you as a key member of the team. I'll also understand if you have to make a hard choice and go to Ireland. But I won't be able to hold your job for you. I would like to, but I'll have to bring someone else in to take over your important tasks."

Situation 3: Two of your Millennials are tasked to write a document to be sent to your senior clients. The work they turn in is plain awful: sketchy, incomplete, inconsistent, filled with writing problems. What feedback do you give and how do you get the document rewritten correctly without doing it yourself?

Millennials don't always distinguish between business writing and the kind of steam-of-consciousness prose they pour onto blogs, wikis, and Web sites. On the other hand, they are often well-educated and have at least seen examples of "old school" writing. Rely on this background to guide them in the revision process: "Great ideas here, but you need to recast them into a form our clients expect. Here's a model. Look it over carefully, then rework your material so that the end product looks and reads like the model. I'm completely confident that you can do it."

Situation 4: As a general habit, Millennials in your office abuse your managerial time by coming to you too often with ideas, questions, observations, and just ordinary chat. How do you handle the propensity of Millennials to want to be pals with the boss?

Sometimes you feel like locking your office door to anyone under twenty-five. They just don't seem to understand how busy you are—or how aimless and rambling their visits appear to be. From the Millennial's point of view, of course, the visit to your office is a special invitation (to you) to join the Millennial club, at least on an emeritus basis. The visit to your office is probably intended to bring you up to speed, albeit in a rapid-fire, disorganized way, on the interloper's thoughts and feelings along with some general info on office politics, Millennial style. To the extent that you can stretch your calendar to include these visits, welcome them as your chance to get to know your younger employees. Ten minutes spent listening in the middle of a hectic workday can do much to build mutual trust, showing that you "get it" and that Millennials are free to share their perspectives with you.

Situation 5: You send out employees by themselves or in small teams to give presentations to potential clients. So far you haven't sent out any of your Millennials by themselves for such work. What is it that you worry about in sending these young employees out to represent the company in front of the client? How can those worries be resolved?

"He doesn't trust us." That's the rumor flashing around the office as it becomes apparent that only old-school employees get to make client presentations. In fact, the Millennials are partly right; you do have your deep reservations about how a hip, kaleidoscopic presentation by a Millennial will suit a banker expecting PowerPoint logic and pace. But look closely at your clients and their needs. Not every client is closing in on retirement and hard of hearing. Some, in fact, may be closer to the interests and style of your Millennials than to your own presentation preferences. Take a risk and show some trust by sending a Millennial team to make a presentation (perhaps a low-stakes one) to these kinds of clients. Let the results guide your further use of Millennials as presenters.

Situation 6: You look at your financial picture for the coming year and realize that you can't give much more than cost-of-living raises to the several Millennials in the company. You resolve to be creative in figuring out other inducements and motivations to keep them with you and keep them working hard. What are some of these incentives?

Millennials hate being conned. They have grown up with an Internet chock full of deceptions ("You're the one millionth visitor to this site!") and false promises. Perhaps more than any other recent generation of employees, they crave straight talk, trust, and honesty. In the case of your financial dilemma, sit them down en masse and explain the situation. Let them ask questions. Even more important, let them make suggestions on non-financial add-ons that would make their jobs more enjoyable and fulfilling. You may be pleasantly surprised to learn that what they want (computer games at lunch hour?) may be quite inexpensive to provide. They will appreciate and respond to the trust you demonstrate in making them part of the solution.

Situation 7: You find yourself giving much more mentoring time to one of your Millennial workers than the others. Frankly, this one worker needs your time and help more than do the others. But you worry that the highly social group of Millennials in your office will feel that one of them is getting special treatment while the others are being ignored. How do you handle this situation?

Millennials would rather have matters out in the open than whispered behind their backs. Maintain trust with your workforce, therefore, by first meeting privately with the employee you are mentoring. Make sure that he or she accepts your necessity to "go public" in the office with the mentoring program, including the fact that no stigma is attached to it. Once they grasp the picture, Millennials are reasonably sure to accept individual differences and needs without much fanfare—probably with a yawn. Again, however, they will value the trust you have demonstrated by making them aware of the full situation.

Situation 8: You pair up one of your Millennials with a middle-aged employee who has been with you for several years. They are supposed to operate as a team, but within days the older employee (according to the Millennial) "is always telling me what to do" and "making all the decisions." The older employee says, "She's not capable of getting one thing done at a time. We discuss goals, but then she's off in a thousand directions. She doesn't know how to finish anything." You wanted the Millennial to get some valuable experience working with the older employee, but how do you keep their differences from undercutting office morale and hurting productivity?

Millennials can become extraordinarily frustrated with old-school workers, and vice versa. If you tell the old-school employee to "cut the new guy some slack," he or she may feel that you are playing favorites. If you tell the Millennial to "shape up or ship out," you run the risk of losing your younger workers in droves. Therefore, provide intervention between the two employees. Talk to them separately (and patiently) about the obvious style differences they each bring to their work experience. Make sure they understand that their approach, while valued, isn't the only approach. Then meet with them together, preferably in an atmosphere that doesn't make it seem they have been "called on the carpet." You can call the meeting a planning session for their next team project. In the meeting, express your trust in the competence of both employees. Get them to discuss their working relationship, including any tensions that have emerged. Don't judge these tensions to be right or wrong. Involve the two employees in a problem-solving discussion where they decide (rather than having you dictate) how they will handle disagreements and style differences when they occur in the future, as they surely will.

In summary, Millennials are a new breed of employee deserving careful forethought when it comes to management strategy. This thinking and planning is not optional for business leaders, especially when they consider that Millennials will comprise the majority of the workforce within the decade. The key to motivating and managing Millennials lies in expressing trust and expecting it in return.

Chapter Nine

Trust in Global Business

"The leaders who work most effectively, it seems to me, never say 'I.' And that's not because they have trained themselves not to say 'I.' They don't think 'I.' They think 'we'; they think 'team.' They understand their job to be to make the team function. They accept responsibility and don't sidestep it, but 'we' get the credit. This is what creates trust, what enables you to get the task done."
Peter Drucker, management expert

As they outsource jobs and establish international operations, American companies face an increasing problem: how to overcome cultural barriers in establishing trust relationships with trading nations around the world. Virtual teams within such global companies have their own trust challenges: Mr. Takahashi based in Japan must be encouraged to speak freely and frankly with his team counterpart, Ms. Singh, in India, and their mutual colleague, Mr. Wong, in China. The process of leaping over cultural barriers isn't achieved by an executive memo urging candor and trust. Instead, these must-have attributes of successful global companies come about through understanding and respecting cultural differences.

Let's not make the mistake of thinking about the efforts to achieve candor and trust in intercultural business as a phenomenon only of the early twenty-first century. In fact, people of different cultures have been reaching out to do business with one another for five thousand years or more. When trust ran high in such dealings, increased prosperity ensued. When trust failed, the result was most often war.

Viewed against the backdrop of previous world and regional conflicts, trust lately has made remarkable gains among nations. With the advent of the euro currency throughout European Union countries, formerly adversarial cultures are putting aside historical prejudices for the sake of advantageous business and social relations. A related development fostering peaceful interactions is the increasing presence of one country's business ventures on the soil of another country. Japanese, Korean, French, German, and Swedish automobile manufacturers have all opened manufacturing plants and assembly facilities in the United States. At the same time, U.S. business icons such as IBM, General Motors, Boeing, Johnson & Johnson, and Coke are powerful and popular employers and business names around the world. An increasing percentage of U.S. real estate is owned by foreign investors, as are our government bonds. Even the Seattle Mariners baseball team is partially owned by the Japanese game giant Nintendo.

What makes these sorts of international business relationships possible? Even in the absence of binding, efficient international laws, companies have forged trust bonds that allow trade to flourish. Take trade with China, for example. U.S. companies conducting business with China at present have no ready access to a world court willing to adjudicate all claims of contract violation, copyright infringement, or other business problems. (There is a World Court in the Hague, of course. The point here is that companies have little luck lining up to sue one another internationally with the same efficiency that they do domestically.) Trust relationships, not laws, make up the social and financial glue that hold these trade deals together.

The key issues for this chapter, therefore, are to locate what forces, attitudes, or events tend to break trust among intercultural trading partners, and what "trust builders" can be established and encouraged for the sake of intercultural trade.

Breaking or Building Trust in Intercultural Trading Relations

Why do deals that seemed so promising and profitable often fall apart between intercultural trading partners? The list of factors is long indeed:
- Contractual failure. One or both of the trading partners fails to live up to their end of the bargain.
- Product or service failure. A product or service of sufficient quality to go to market in the manufacturer's country fails the safety standards of the trading partner's country. For example, lead in the paint of Chinese toys has caused a massive and expensive recall for Mattel.
- Political interference. World events change market conditions so that the trading partners cannot buy or sell in one another's countries. Goods from Cuba, for example, do not enter the U.S. legally, or vice versa.
- Attitude shifts. The buying public in one country may "get mad" at another culture or country, with devastating effects on its imported goods. French wine, for example, took a market nosedive when many Americans disapproved of the foreign policies of France.
- Economic nationalism and isolationism. Waves of "buy it at home" sentiment can lock foreign goods and services out of a domestic market. The "Made in the U.S.A." label became the rallying cry for U.S. textile workers who saw their jobs disappearing to cheaper foreign workers.
- Monetary barriers. The stability of their respective currencies must be assured for intercultural business partners to enter into trustworthy business relations. For many years, the instability of the Chinese yuan and the Russian ruble made trading relations with these countries problematic.

- Lack of trained workers. Trade relations between would-be partners rely on the presence of a labor force in each country able to do the jobs required. When computer manufacturers in the U.S. were seeking partners in Mexico for assembly work, they had to first provide extensive training for workers whose previous work experience had been light manufacturing or agrarian.

Many of these factors are beyond the control of companies themselves, but even in the worst of circumstances and against all odds, companies have often been able to hold intercultural trade relations together. In large part, this achievement is due to at least six "Trust Builders":

- Companies engage one another with tolerance. They do not insist on any specific values or behaviors as being universally right.
- Employees at all levels in partner companies are trained to be flexible and accepting of differences in values, beliefs, standards, and mores.
- Employees know they must be sensitive to verbal nuances and nonverbal signals.
- Companies recognize that knowledge of religious, cultural, business, and social practices of other cultures is a necessity.
- Companies prepare for the fact that within a foreign culture many different values and preferences may coexist.
- Mutual interest in a potentially profitable commercial relationship compels parties to learn new ways of doing business.

Obviously, within the scope of this book on trust we cannot investigate all intercultural factors that make or break trust in trade abroad. But we can explore areas where trust relationships are stressed in intercultural trade. In these arenas, the customs and expectations of both partners may differ widely, requiring a meeting of the minds as well as healthy doses of trust and candor to keep business humming.

Trust in the Agreement Process

To a U.S. businessperson, an agreement completed with a signed contract is almost sacred. To break the contract means to be legally liable, not to mention the damage to one's integrity and reputation. In the Middle East, however, a contract may be viewed somewhat suspiciously as just a piece of paper that can be undone as easily as the paper can be destroyed. The true agreement for these cultures may be constituted by a handshake between the parties after deliberate and thorough discussions over many cups of coffee. For some Arab business leaders, the presentation of a formalized contract for signatures may be taken as an affront or a lack of trust. Throughout the countries of the former Soviet Union and in Greece, the signing of a contract (no matter what the contract language) is often taken as the opening gambit in a give-and-take of business terms that continues throughout the business relationship. In China, a formalized contract is struck more for the comfort level of the Western business partner than for binding legal purposes. Chinese business relies on mutual trust more than a document for business understandings. The understandings and mutual respect earned through many long conversations among the principals, often over meals, are far more influential in assuring compliance to business terms than a paper contract. Many U.S. construction firms that have embarked on major projects abroad have found that their foreign contractual partners look upon their carefully worded, legally reviewed contracts as just the beginning of negotiations, not the end.

Trust When Ethics Differ

The ethical standards and practices of one culture may seem repugnant to or may be patently illegal in another culture. For example, under-the-table payment to an individual or group to secure a contract would be termed a bribe in the U.S. In many other cultures, such a monetary gesture is not illegal at all and is viewed as a form of commission for services rendered. Certain actions or comments in a U.S. office may be called sexual harassment and are both unethical and illegal. In other workplaces, the same interactions may not be taken seriously at all. Trust allows a dialogue to take place in which business partners come to terms with ethical differences and forge working relations that recognize those differences.

Trust Involving Differing Views on Male-Female Relations

What some cultures perceive as the natural and historical subordination of women to men strikes many Americans as unfortunate and unjust. The ethical and political issues involved come to a head when a U.S. businesswoman faces hard choices: Will she be effective in doing business in cultures that suppress women? Can she do so in good conscience? The answers to these difficult questions are deeply personal and situational. But three trends have emerged in recent years:

1. Businesswomen are visiting sexually hostile cultures in increasing numbers. They are often accorded respect and a range of latitude not given to native women in those cultures.
2. When businesswomen anticipate problems due to sexual assumptions, they can prepare in advance by establishing their professional status with their foreign clients through correspondence, telephone conversations, and mutual acquaintances.
3. Women sometimes make initial business contacts in such cultures in the company of male colleagues, who then withdraw as the business relationship develops.

A favorite tenet of cultural relativism is that mores and customs are neither right nor wrong, just different. But in the case of sexual discrimination (or racial or ethic discrimination), cultures, like individuals, can simply be wrongheaded. Attitudes change, however, as women assert themselves as professionals equally capable of doing business. Attitudes also change as economically disadvantaged cultures observe that enterprising trading partners come from cultures respecting women.

Trust and Interpersonal Behavior

No matter how much we study another culture, it is unlikely in the short term that we will be able to abide by all its subtleties in human interaction. Trust is the great forgiver in these circumstances. Employees on both sides of the cultural divide realize that their counterparts' hearts are in the right place. They may inadvertently do strange or even offensive things from the point of view of another culture, but they are trusted not to mean anything by it. For example, typical U.S. attitudes toward touching are vastly different from that of many other cultures in the world. It is not unusual in Europe or the Middle East to see two men or two women walking together with hands clasped or even encircling a shoulder or waist. Such a sight remains as unusual here as seeing two men greet each other with a kiss on one cheek or both—a relatively common sight in many other cultures.

Discussion between a manager and a subordinate in the United States may occur with each in a very relaxed posture. They might be drinking coffee. If the manager is a man (or, for that matter, a women in a pantsuit), a foot may be casually hooked over an empty chair or planted on a nearby tabletop. Not so in the Middle East, where crossing one's legs or facing the soles of one's shoes toward another individual is a sign of rudeness. In many cultures, certainly throughout Asia and Europe, the subordinate is expected to be virtually at attention when in conference with a superior. For example, keeping your hands in your pockets when addressing your German or Austrian boss is just not done.

In the United States we are sometimes concerned when the other person does not look us in the eye or seems otherwise visually evasive. We suspect discomfort on the person's part, and perhaps a lack of honesty or integrity. In Japan, a businessperson may interpret a lack of respect if another individual does look them directly in the eye. Such eye contact may well signal defiance, hostility, or impertinence.

U.S. businesspeople have no hesitancy, when asked, to list their accomplishments and other status markers. In much of Asia such behavior would seem out of place and in bad taste. One's *meishi,* or presentation of professional status, is accomplished in the ritual of presenting one's business card (usually with accompanying translation on the reverse side of the card for the convenience of the person receiving it). When accepting a business card, the person is expected in Asian cultures to pay attention to it for a few moments, to comment appropriately on the person's accomplishments, to thank the person for offering the card, and to give a card in response. For both parties, the presentation of the card is usually made with a slight bow, and always with both hands holding the card.

It would be culturally unwise for an American manager to single out one Chinese, Korean, or Japanese employee in the presence of his or her coworkers for extended praise. While common practice in the U.S., such spotlighting of the individual would be embarrassing for all concerned in many Asian business cultures. "The nail that protrudes must be knocked down," goes the Japanese saying.

Trust in Language Misunderstandings

In the same way that companies struggle to get it right in interpersonal relations, they also work hard (and spend large advertising budgets) trying to communicate to another culture correctly. Often that effort misfires, sometimes hilariously so.

Trust in the good intentions of a foreign partner is the primary force that covers the embarrassment of a language disaster. A group of Hispanic ad agencies in Los Angeles have formed an organization called Merito: The Society for Excellence in Hispanic Advertising. The organization has as its mission the "elimination of misunderstandings, bad translations, and bad advertising by non-Hispanics to the Hispanic market." The group sites examples such as the slogan used by Braniff Airways: "Travel on leather." The Spanish word for "leather" *(cuero)* also means "naked," with the resulting message, "Travel naked." Examples abound from other cultures as well. "Come alive with Pepsi" was inadvertently translated into German as "Come out of the grave with Pepsi." In Asia, "Body by Fisher," stamped on U.S.-exported autos, was read as "Corpse by Fisher." Common U.S. sayings such as "The spirit is willing but the flesh is weak" become in Russian "The ghost is ready but the meat is rotten." These are extreme examples, of course, but they point out the care American managers must take in relying on translation to communicate their key messages.

Trust That Overcomes Differences in Business Mannerisms and Expectations

While an American or Briton might feel obliged to crack a joke or two during a meeting or presentation, or an Italian or French worker indulge in witticism, other cultures frown upon such levity in the business environment. Humor, in short, is an expected icebreaker for many cultures, but for others it is both unexpected and inappropriate.

The most marked difference between business communications in Korea and the U.S. is the difference between American objectivity and Korean subjectivity. For businesspeople in the U.S., relationships and personal feelings (both positive and negative) are to be set aside in favor of impartial and dispassionate logic. For Koreans, sincerity and commitment to individuals is the basis for business dealings. Business is transacted by two people, not by the firms they represent.

Business meetings in Italy are usually unstructured and informal. They do not follow pre-established agendas and participants may (and do) come and go as the meeting progresses. Anyone may speak at any time and eloquence, not status, is the key to earning an audience. Decisions implemented later by the company may have no bearing at all on those made in the meeting.

In Vietnam, the boss is the boss—anytime, anywhere. In the U.S., an executive away from the office can relax and pursue leisure in any way he or she chooses. In Vietnam, leisure must be pursued according to one's station in business and in life generally. Executives in Vietnam would never eat in simple, small restaurants because the food is good; they must go only to first-rate, elegant restaurants to maintain image and reputation (their own and their company's).

Latin Americans tend to view all of life holistically, and this perspective applies to business relations as well. Whereas a good conversation between U.S. businesspeople is one that is focused, task-oriented, and concise, one between Latin Americans is more likely to touch on various topics, to consider each subject from all possible dimensions, and to move only indirectly toward a conclusion.

Self-Knowledge as a Basis for Trusting Others: Facing U.S. Values

Socrates advised, "Know thyself" as the first necessary step in preparing to know and trust others. By understanding what makes us tick, we are in a better position to understand why foreign partners may experience initial or long-term difficulties getting to know and trust us. Too often, we see the other party as the "different" one. The following summary of American values demonstrates that we, too, bring our peculiarities to the trading table. Achieving trust with a foreign partner inevitably involves helping them understand where we're coming from with regard to core values. We can't do so unless we call those values to mind.

Ironically, an American just returning from a two-week trip to France may find it easier to answer the question, "What do the French value?" than the question, "What do Americans value?" The differences of viewpoint and approach to life and business seem clear to us after only a short exposure to another culture, whereas our own cultural experience—in effect, the cultural air we breathe—remains foggy and undefined.

By taking time to look squarely at our own cultural assumptions and beliefs, we equip ourselves to find points of similarity and difference with other cultures. We may also become more humble and less apt to claim cultural superiority, for a close look at dominant U.S. values at least raises some ethical questions. In the following list, some of the suggested values may not be yours. Judge, however, whether you believe these values to be generally shared by American culture. To trust you as a business partner, foreign managers do not necessarily have to agree with these values, but they should understand them.

- Personal control over the environment. In the United States, people consider it normal and proper that human beings control nature. That may mean changing the size of a mountain, the location of a lake, the direction or even the existence of a river, and perhaps the genetic structure of a living organism. Most of the world's population think that such changes are fraught with danger. Fate, they believe, plays a powerful role in human life. Natural structures and forces are the face of fate: immutable, unyielding, and not to be manipulated by mere humans.
- Change. People in the U.S. usually feel change is a good thing, something that signals progress and brings renewed interest and excitement to life.

Change is associated with development, growth, and advancement. Older cultures, however, often view change as disruptive and destructive. The established order, for all its flaws, is usually preferable in these cultures to the unknown and unpredictable results of new beginnings, revolutions, and social experiments.

- Control of time. Time exerts both control and pressure on people in the United States. Time here is valuable and highly prized; not to observe time commitments is interpreted as a sign of discourtesy to others, lack of ambition, and general slovenliness. Other cultures worry less about punctuality and deadlines. Time is viewed as a medium, not as a constraint, in which people pursue business activities and personal relationships.
- Equality. By our Constitution and tradition, we view individuals as created equal; we value equality as an important civic and social goal. But in much of the world, rank, status, and authority are viewed as part and parcel of everyday life, including business life. To many individuals in other cultures, knowing who they are and where they fit in the various strata of their society offers a sense of security and identification.
- Individualism and privacy. People in the United States feel strongly that they are individuals who deserve and expect distinct treatment for their unique viewpoints and qualities. In other cultures, especially where space is at a premium in homes, offices, and workplaces, the concept of individualism and the need for privacy is of less importance. One's membership in the group and one's flexibility in meeting group goals take precedence.
- Self-help. Americans take pride in making it on their own. If someone inherits wealth, that person downplays it and focuses instead on efforts to make his or her own contribution to personal welfare. The same is not true of many other cultures, where the self-made man or

woman may be given much less respect than the person endowed with wealth or position by birthright or class.
- Competition and free enterprise. Americans value competition and stress it in the classroom, on the sports field, and in the boardroom. But in societies that value cooperation, the intense competitiveness of the United States is not easy to comprehend. "Getting ahead" for the individual is seen as essentially anti-social in nature and destructive of larger social goals.
- Action and work values. Americans work long and hard. Their workdays are planned, with work activities scheduled weeks or months in advance. We become so involved in and defined by work activities that we become workaholics. Many cultures consider such monomaniacal focus on work both inhuman and destructive. Meditation, recreation, and human relations are valued above the additional wealth that could be achieved by a heavier workload.
- Directness, openness, and honesty. People from other countries often look upon Americans as being blunt, perhaps even unfeeling. But people in the U.S. may pride themselves on "telling it like it is." This direct approach is difficult to understand for an individual who comes from a society where saving face is important and where communicating unpopular judgments or information may be dangerous. We may lose interest in people—"wimps"—who hint at what they intend rather than stating the situation directly. By contrast, members of other cultures often lose trust in us because of our directness.
- Materialism. Most people in other cultures perceive Americans as being more materialistic than we perceive ourselves. We look upon our cars, appliances, homes, TVs, computers, and other material items as our just rewards for hard work. In contrast, many

others see us as partners in a demented love affair with the things of this world, as if amassing an ever-growing collection of such material items would guarantee contentment and enlightenment.

Candor in Writing and Speaking for International Audiences

Achieving open, spontaneous, and accurate business communications with foreign individuals—"Let's chat the way we do in America"—isn't solely a matter of good intentions. In fact, most cultures are more formal than the United States in both writing and speaking. Foreign individuals at first may have great difficulty "letting their hair down" to communicate in frank, unguarded ways.

Consider, for example, the use of titles in global communications. U.S. businesspeople should use titles when addressing their counterparts in the rest of the world. Unless you have a longstanding relationship with someone abroad and have already used his or her first name in casual conversation, always use a surname and title.

Opening paragraphs of a letter in international correspondence are usually formal or introductory. Brief comments on the weather, a previous trip or association, or a non-controversial international event or incident are quite appropriate as ice-breakers. Giving best wishes for the time of year (the New Year in Asia, for example) or season is also common and welcomed. Sensitive factors such as late payments, behavior of representatives, and errors or delays in shipping should be handled with great delicacy and tact.

Business documents in various countries differ not only in form, but also in pattern of organization, tone, and level of detail. German documents, for example, are often heavily detailed, while

Latin American documents emphasize a polite, refined style and generalized concepts. Reports for Japanese associates must be prepared with formal, honorific openings. Casual analogies and other non-business-related information get cut from the reports and proposals sent to British colleagues.

Even when you try to follow the style and tone of the documents written by native businesspeople in Latin America, Asia, and Europe, your "Americanness" will still show. Some of that is certainly acceptable. Intercultural readers, whether located inside the U.S. or abroad, expect American communications to show the features of American document conventions. Nonetheless, shrewd intercultural communicators still try hard to shape their writing habits and assumptions toward the communication needs and expectations of their readers. As a case in point, many European cultures expect significant business correspondence to end with two signatures—the signatures of both the letter writer and his or her superior. Therefore, to get a more positive reaction from a European reader, the American letter writer may decide to use two signatures.

An American writer may even have to learn when not to write at all. As reported in separate studies by Michael Yoshino and William Ouchi, Japanese companies don't use written communication for routine business matters as much as American companies do. If an American writer communicates solely by memo, a Japanese reader may tend to treat the message as being inappropriately serious or important, calling a meeting, for example, to discuss the implications of the memo. Instead, alternate channels of communication should be chosen: a conference telephone call, perhaps, or a face-to-face meeting in person or via teleconference with selected decision makers.

A final example involves the use of first names. In American correspondence, it is common after the first two or three business contacts to begin addressing the reader by his or her first name. This practice is generally taken in our culture to be a sign of friendliness and trust. In Germany, however, business readers look upon the use of first names as a sign of inappropriate chumminess bordering on disrespect.

Establishing and Maintaining Trust through Listening

Just as writing and speaking forms and approaches differ from culture to culture, so do listening habits and outward manifestations of attention. In Western cultures, intense listening is usually signaled by sustained eye contact given by the audience to the speaker along with responsive facial expressions (smiles, nods, and so forth). In many Asian cultures, however, the same degree of intense listening may be indicated by an averted gaze, with little animation of facial features. Western speakers new to such cultures must be careful not to judge the attention or interest level of an Asian audience by Western signs of listening.

In virtually all Western business environments, it would be considered impolite for an audience member to mill about, whisper to others, or leave the room entirely (except for emergencies) during a presentation. Not so in Japan and some other Asian business cultures, where it is commonplace for audience members in a business presentation to exchange notes, talk quietly in small groups, and come and go freely from the room as the presentation continues. From a Western presenter's point of view, this behavior may be misunderstood as a lack of interest on the part of audience members. But from a Japanese perspective, it is not necessary for all members of a decision-making team to be present for all portions of the presentation. The team trusts its members to gather the information needed from the presentation, even if no one team member hears the entire presentation from start to finish.

Another listening problem for a Westerner is often presented by Chinese hosts, for whom it is perfectly acceptable at meals or meetings including a Westerner to break into prolonged conversations in Mandarin or Cantonese. Even if a translator is present, these conversations typically go untranslated. The Westerner is left wondering whether to stare dumbly at his or her hosts, deep in Chinese conversation, to look to the translator for help, or to look elsewhere until the hosts again direct conversation to the Westerner in English or through the translator. Probably this last option is the best. The Westerner's visible signs of comfort during moments of untranslated conversation will come as a relief for Chinese business hosts. At the same time, the experience should alert the Westerner to feelings of being left out, feelings often encountered by Asian visitors to U.S. meetings and meals, where English buzzes on with little if any translation effort.

Cultures also have different conventions governing how long audience members are typically willing to listen before offering reaction or input; where and when it is appropriate to listen to a sustained business presentation; and what they expect to hear in such presentations.

Building Trust by the Way You Speak

At the same time you are preparing for a meeting with a foreign business relation, investigating the useful foreign phrases you will use to ease communication, remember to examine your own ways of speaking in an intercultural context as an important component of establishing trust. You can aid your hosts in understanding your business communications in three key ways:

1. avoiding slang and idioms
2. slowing down your speech
3. checking your listener's understanding of what you are saying

For the sake of clear business dealings abroad, try to become aware of words and phrases that probably will be misunderstood in your international business dealings. Learn to cut out slang and idioms, including local or regional colloquial expressions. Robert Bell, an international magnetic resonance specialist, comments, "When I travel to business meetings abroad, I have to remember that my ordinary mode of friendly conversation contains many idioms (such as 'right on the money') that foreign colleagues will find strange and uninterpretable. I remind myself to speak 'plain vanilla English' around those who don't know American English well."

An American manager wrote the following sentence to a foreign businessperson with limited English skills: "By the way, I've shipped the computer order we discussed last week." The American manager was shocked to receive a telex from his foreign client: "What is the 'the way' you refer to? Urgent to know." American English is rich in such easy-to-use idioms and expressions, with *Barron's Pocket Guide to Clichés* listing more than one thousand of them.

Eliminating your use of idiomatic expressions is just one way to improve your communication with business connections abroad. To help your listener, adjust the pace of your speaking to match the rate of comprehension of your foreign host. You will often do business with men and women who have, through hard work, acquired quite a bit of fluency in English. However, if you rush ahead at the same speaking pace you would use with a native speaker, you unintentionally dash these people's efforts to communicate with you. Before leaving for an international trip, practice slowing down your speech without sounding patronizing. Look directly at the person to whom you are speaking so that he or she can see the words as they form on your lips and notice your facial and hand gestures.

To ensure that your message is being communicated clearly, check for comprehension. Some Americans, when speaking to foreign persons, frown quizzically as a visual way of asking, "Are you following me?" Try not to use the frown in this way. Unfortunately, this puzzled look will often be misinterpreted as anger, criticism, or impatience. Instead, when you want to check for comprehension, raise your eyebrows and give an inquiring smile. That visual gesture will produce either a nod of comprehension from your foreign friend or an indication that he or she has not understood. Learn to check often (in a polite way) to see whether your listener is comprehending. In a telephone conversation, for example, pause to ask, "Am I being clear?" or "Do you understand?" or simply "O.K.?"

In face-to-face conversations, including teleconferences, do not mistake a courteous smile on your listener's face or a nod as a sign of complete comprehension, and certainly not of complete agreement. Particularly in Asian and Latin American cultures, your listener will give you a smile simply as a polite gesture. Asian listeners may even nod and "yes" (*hai*) repeatedly in an effort to show respect to you. All the while, they may almost entirely misunderstand what you are saying. Good barometers of such misunderstanding are the eyes. Watch to see whether your listener's eyes respond to your words. If you notice a glazed, lost look, back up and begin again in a simpler fashion. Another helpful technique is to politely ask the other party to repeat what he or she understood you to say. In working with a translator, this process is called "back translation."

In all the foregoing ways, Americans can encourage trust on the part of their foreign business partners and welcome reciprocal trust. Especially when it comes to intercultural relationships, lasting trust is not established or maintained by any single mantra or silver bullet. The trust-building process requires knowledge about and interest in the dozens of ways in which cultures differ.

Chapter Ten

Measuring Dimensions of Workplace Trust

"People have at their very fingertips, at the tips of their brains, tremendous amounts of tacit knowledge, which are not captured in our computer systems or on paper. Trust is the utility through which this knowledge flows."
     Karen Stephenson, author, Quantum Theory of Trust

This chapter contains sample surveys for evaluating trust across key organizational levels at companies. We have identified nine exchange points where low levels of trust consistently impede the candid and accurate exchange of information and ideas among key work groups. Conversely, high levels of trust at these exchange points generally direct the way to increased collaboration. These instruments are most effective when a two-way connection is established: employees providing data on trust attitudes and behaviors in relation to the manager(s), and the manager(s) simultaneously providing data on trust attitudes and behaviors in relation to their employees.

When used throughout an organization or a division or work unit, the full battery of surveys provides a wealth of diagnostic and prescriptive data for the following dimensions of trust relationships:

- Employee to employee
- Employee to manager
- Manager to employee
- Manager to manager
- Employee to senior leadership

- Senior leadership to employee
- Manager to senior leadership
- Senior leadership to manager
- Senior leadership to senior leadership

The completed assessment tools form the foundation for building a credibility map for each company. We validate the exchange point data from the assessment tools with targeted focus groups, interviews, and evaluation of independent surveys of the workforce. The credibility map visually identifies low, medium, and high levels of trust in key areas of the company. The creation of a complete credibility map involves close consultation between the authors and an organization. Initial findings, however, can be estimated by administering the questionnaires provided in this chapter, then comparing results for separate groups of survey-takers. How, for example, was a question answered by your managers in the Manager to Employee survey versus a parallel question on the Employee to Manager survey? Each question in these instruments can be evaluated across survey-taking groups for purposes of such comparison. Where results differ significantly, a credibility gap has been located. You have thus discovered a variance in trust that may be affecting the productivity of your organization.

Evaluating and rebuilding trust is not a one-size-fits-all endeavor, but rather must be shaped to the contours of company's history, corporate culture, competitive pressures, and other factors. We use the exchange point data and credibility map to identify specifically where trust lags and ways to rebuild levels of trust in that particular part of that particular company. At the organizational level, we use the assessment tools to evaluate the three building blocks of workplace trust: accessibility of information, ideas, and people; transparency of structures and processes; and visibility of candor. We evaluate the building blocks of trust at the individual employee level—assertiveness, cohesion, and candor—to more closely target approaches for individuals and work groups.

The four assessment tools included here are meant as a guide on initiating the process of assessing levels of trust within a company. All surveys should be kept strictly confidential to encourage candor and high levels of responses from different groups of employees. Results of the surveys should be presented with no information identifying any of the respondents other than job category and job level. Surveys are also customized to fit the organizational structure or take into account unique circumstances occurring at a specific exchange point.

Sample Surveys

Employee to Employee
Employee to Manager
Manager to Employee
Manager to Senior Leadership

Employee to Employee Survey

1. My fellow employees speak up to provide one another with the information needed to do their jobs well.

Strongly Agree	Agree	Somewhat Agree	Neither Agree Nor Disagree	Somewhat Disagree	Disagree	Strongly Disagree	Not Applicable to Me
○	○	○	○	○	○	○	○

2. My fellow employees communicate truthfully with one another in their written, oral, and online messages.

Strongly Agree	Agree	Somewhat Agree	Neither Agree Nor Disagree	Somewhat Disagree	Disagree	Strongly Disagree	Not Applicable to Me
○	○	○	○	○	○	○	○

3. My fellow employees must often read between the lines to understand what they really mean in their communications to one another.

Strongly Agree	Agree	Somewhat Agree	Neither Agree Nor Disagree	Somewhat Disagree	Disagree	Strongly Disagree	Not Applicable to Me
○	○	○	○	○	○	○	○

4. There is much that my fellow employees are not telling one another about workplace relationships.

Strongly Agree	Agree	Somewhat Agree	Neither Agree Nor Disagree	Somewhat Disagree	Disagree	Strongly Disagree	Not Applicable to Me
○	○	○	○	○	○	○	○

5. My fellow employees tend to make up stories or excuses to one another about work-related problems.

Strongly Agree	Agree	Somewhat Agree	Neither Agree Nor Disagree	Somewhat Disagree	Disagree	Strongly Disagree	Not Applicable to Me
○	○	○	○	○	○	○	○

6. My fellow employees openly discuss their opinions, observations, and suggestions with one another.

Strongly Agree	Agree	Somewhat Agree	Neither Agree Nor Disagree	Somewhat Disagree	Disagree	Strongly Disagree	Not Applicable to Me
○	○	○	○	○	○	○	○

7. My fellow employees trust one another.

Strongly Agree	Agree	Somewhat Agree	Neither Agree Nor Disagree	Somewhat Disagree	Disagree	Strongly Disagree	Not Applicable to Me
○	○	○	○	○	○	○	○

8. My fellow employees make sure to discuss difficult work-related issues with one another.

Strongly Agree	Agree	Somewhat Agree	Neither Agree Nor Disagree	Somewhat Disagree	Disagree	Strongly Disagree	Not Applicable to Me
○	○	○	○	○	○	○	○

9. My fellow employees discuss their opinions and concerns with one another about the company and its business direction.

Strongly Agree	Agree	Somewhat Agree	Neither Agree Nor Disagree	Somewhat Disagree	Disagree	Strongly Disagree	Not Applicable to Me
○	○	○	○	○	○	○	○

10. My fellow employees regularly communicate with one another about their jobs.

Strongly Agree	Agree	Somewhat Agree	Neither Agree Nor Disagree	Somewhat Disagree	Disagree	Strongly Disagree	Not Applicable to Me
○	○	○	○	○	○	○	○

11. My fellow employees tend to distrust one another.

Strongly Agree	Agree	Somewhat Agree	Neither Agree Nor Disagree	Somewhat Disagree	Disagree	Strongly Disagree	Not Applicable to Me
○	○	○	○	○	○	○	○

12. My fellow employees have difficulty telling one another the plain truth about work-related problems.

Strongly Agree	Agree	Somewhat Agree	Neither Agree Nor Disagree	Somewhat Disagree	Disagree	Strongly Disagree	Not Applicable to Me
○	○	○	○	○	○	○	○

13. My fellow employees bring work-related problems to one another's attention quickly.

Strongly Agree	Agree	Somewhat Agree	Neither Agree Nor Disagree	Somewhat Disagree	Disagree	Strongly Disagree	Not Applicable to Me
○	○	○	○	○	○	○	○

14. My fellow employees look at our organization as a high-performing team.

Strongly Agree	Agree	Somewhat Agree	Neither Agree Nor Disagree	Somewhat Disagree	Disagree	Strongly Disagree	Not Applicable to Me
○	○	○	○	○	○	○	○

15. When my fellow employees make a work-related mistake, they discuss it with affected employees.

Strongly Agree	Agree	Somewhat Agree	Neither Agree Nor Disagree	Somewhat Disagree	Disagree	Strongly Disagree	Not Applicable to Me
○	○	○	○	○	○	○	○

16. Work-related performance problems experienced by my fellow employees are usually due to a lack of training.

Strongly Agree | Agree | Somewhat Agree | Neither Agree Nor Disagree | Somewhat Disagree | Disagree | Strongly Disagree | Not Applicable to Me

○ ○ ○ ○ ○ ○ ○ ○

17. My fellow employees tend to blame their own work problems on others.

Strongly Agree | Agree | Somewhat Agree | Neither Agree Nor Disagree | Somewhat Disagree | Disagree | Strongly Disagree | Not Applicable to Me

○ ○ ○ ○ ○ ○ ○ ○

18. My fellow employees spend too much time going over the same messages and directions to one another.

Strongly Agree | Agree | Somewhat Agree | Neither Agree Nor Disagree | Somewhat Disagree | Disagree | Strongly Disagree | Not Applicable to Me

○ ○ ○ ○ ○ ○ ○ ○

19. Lack of information accounts for important work-related problems encountered by my fellow employees on the job.

Strongly Agree | Agree | Somewhat Agree | Neither Agree Nor Disagree | Somewhat Disagree | Disagree | Strongly Disagree | Not Applicable to Me

○ ○ ○ ○ ○ ○ ○ ○

20. My fellow employees rate their working relationship with one another very positively.

Strongly Agree | Agree | Somewhat Agree | Neither Agree Nor Disagree | Somewhat Disagree | Disagree | Strongly Disagree | Not Applicable to Me

○ ○ ○ ○ ○ ○ ○ ○

Employee to Manager Survey

1. I speak up to provide my manager with the information needed to do his or her job well.

Strongly Agree | Agree | Somewhat Agree | Neither Agree Nor Disagree | Somewhat Disagree | Disagree | Strongly Disagree | Not Applicable to Me

○ ○ ○ ○ ○ ○ ○ ○

2. I communicate truthfully with my manger in my written, oral, and online messages.

Strongly Agree | Agree | Somewhat Agree | Neither Agree Nor Disagree | Somewhat Disagree | Disagree | Strongly Disagree | Not Applicable to Me

○ ○ ○ ○ ○ ○ ○ ○

3. My manager must often read between the lines to understand what I really mean in my communications.

Strongly Agree | Agree | Somewhat Agree | Neither Agree Nor Disagree | Somewhat Disagree | Disagree | Strongly Disagree | Not Applicable to Me

○ ○ ○ ○ ○ ○ ○ ○

4. There is much that I am not telling my manager about his or her management skills.

Strongly Agree | Agree | Somewhat Agree | Neither Agree Nor Disagree | Somewhat Disagree | Disagree | Strongly Disagree | Not Applicable to Me

○ ○ ○ ○ ○ ○ ○ ○

5. I tend to make up stories or excuses for work-related problems.

Strongly Agree | Agree | Somewhat Agree | Neither Agree Nor Disagree | Somewhat Disagree | Disagree | Strongly Disagree | Not Applicable to Me

○ ○ ○ ○ ○ ○ ○ ○

6. I openly discuss with my manager my opinions, observations, and suggestions.

Strongly Agree	Agree	Somewhat Agree	Neither Agree Nor Disagree	Somewhat Disagree	Disagree	Strongly Disagree	Not Applicable to Me
○	○	○	○	○	○	○	○

7. I trust my manager.

Strongly Agree	Agree	Somewhat Agree	Neither Agree Nor Disagree	Somewhat Disagree	Disagree	Strongly Disagree	Not Applicable to Me
○	○	○	○	○	○	○	○

8. My manager makes sure to discuss difficult work-related issues with me.

Strongly Agree	Agree	Somewhat Agree	Neither Agree Nor Disagree	Somewhat Disagree	Disagree	Strongly Disagree	Not Applicable to Me
○	○	○	○	○	○	○	○

9. I discuss my opinions and concerns with my manager about the company and its business direction.

Strongly Agree	Agree	Somewhat Agree	Neither Agree Nor Disagree	Somewhat Disagree	Disagree	Strongly Disagree	Not Applicable to Me
○	○	○	○	○	○	○	○

10. I regularly communicate with my manager about my job.

Strongly Agree	Agree	Somewhat Agree	Neither Agree Nor Disagree	Somewhat Disagree	Disagree	Strongly Disagree	Not Applicable to Me
○	○	○	○	○	○	○	○

11. My manager trusts me.

Strongly Agree	Agree	Somewhat Agree	Neither Agree Nor Disagree	Somewhat Disagree	Disagree	Strongly Disagree	Not Applicable to Me
○	○	○	○	○	○	○	○

12. I have difficulty telling my manager the plain truth about work-related problems.

Strongly Agree	Agree	Somewhat Agree	Neither Agree Nor Disagree	Somewhat Disagree	Disagree	Strongly Disagree	Not Applicable to Me
○	○	○	○	○	○	○	○

13. I bring work-related problems to my manager's attention quickly.

Strongly Agree	Agree	Somewhat Agree	Neither Agree Nor Disagree	Somewhat Disagree	Disagree	Strongly Disagree	Not Applicable to Me
○	○	○	○	○	○	○	○

14. I look at our organization as a high-performing team.

Strongly Agree	Agree	Somewhat Agree	Neither Agree Nor Disagree	Somewhat Disagree	Disagree	Strongly Disagree	Not Applicable to Me
○	○	○	○	○	○	○	○

15. When my manager makes a work-related mistake, he or she discusses it with affected employees.

Strongly Agree	Agree	Somewhat Agree	Neither Agree Nor Disagree	Somewhat Disagree	Disagree	Strongly Disagree	Not Applicable to Me
○	○	○	○	○	○	○	○

16. Work-related performance problems I experience are usually due to a lack of training.

Strongly Agree	Agree	Somewhat Agree	Neither Agree Nor Disagree	Somewhat Disagree	Disagree	Strongly Disagree	Not Applicable to Me
○	○	○	○	○	○	○	○

17. I tend to blame my own work problems on others.

Strongly Agree	Agree	Somewhat Agree	Neither Agree Nor Disagree	Somewhat Disagree	Disagree	Strongly Disagree	Not Applicable to Me
○	○	○	○	○	○	○	○

18. My manager spends too much time going over the same messages and directions to one employee.

Strongly Agree	Agree	Somewhat Agree	Neither Agree Nor Disagree	Somewhat Disagree	Disagree	Strongly Disagree	Not Applicable to Me
○	○	○	○	○	○	○	○

19. Lack of information accounts for important work-related problems I encounter on the job.

Strongly Agree	Agree	Somewhat Agree	Neither Agree Nor Disagree	Somewhat Disagree	Disagree	Strongly Disagree	Not Applicable to Me
○	○	○	○	○	○	○	○

20. I rate my working relationship with my manager very positively.

Strongly Agree	Agree	Somewhat Agree	Neither Agree Nor Disagree	Somewhat Disagree	Disagree	Strongly Disagree	Not Applicable to Me
○	○	○	○	○	○	○	○

Manager to Employee Survey

1. My employees speak up to provide me with the information I need to do my job well.

Strongly Agree	Agree	Somewhat Agree	Neither Agree Nor Disagree	Somewhat Disagree	Disagree	Strongly Disagree	Not Applicable to Me
○	○	○	○	○	○	○	○

2. My employees communicate truthfully to me in their written, oral, and online messages.

Strongly Agree	Agree	Somewhat Agree	Neither Agree Nor Disagree	Somewhat Disagree	Disagree	Strongly Disagree	Not Applicable to Me
○	○	○	○	○	○	○	○

3. To understand what my employees really mean, I must read between the lines in their communications.

Strongly Agree	Agree	Somewhat Agree	Neither Agree Nor Disagree	Somewhat Disagree	Disagree	Strongly Disagree	Not Applicable to Me
○	○	○	○	○	○	○	○

4. There is much that my employees are not telling me about my management skills.

Strongly Agree	Agree	Somewhat Agree	Neither Agree Nor Disagree	Somewhat Disagree	Disagree	Strongly Disagree	Not Applicable to Me
○	○	○	○	○	○	○	○

5. My employees tend to make up stories or excuses for work-related problems.

Strongly Agree	Agree	Somewhat Agree	Neither Agree Nor Disagree	Somewhat Disagree	Disagree	Strongly Disagree	Not Applicable to Me
○	○	○	○	○	○	○	○

6. My employees openly discuss with me their opinions, observations, and suggestions.

Strongly Agree	Agree	Somewhat Agree	Neither Agree Nor Disagree	Somewhat Disagree	Disagree	Strongly Disagree	Not Applicable to Me
○	○	○	○	○	○	○	○

7. My employees trust me.

Strongly Agree	Agree	Somewhat Agree	Neither Agree Nor Disagree	Somewhat Disagree	Disagree	Strongly Disagree	Not Applicable to Me
○	○	○	○	○	○	○	○

8. I make sure to discuss difficult work-related issues with my employees.

Strongly Agree	Agree	Somewhat Agree	Neither Agree Nor Disagree	Somewhat Disagree	Disagree	Strongly Disagree	Not Applicable to Me
○	○	○	○	○	○	○	○

9. My employees discuss their opinions and concerns with me about the company and its business direction.

Strongly Agree	Agree	Somewhat Agree	Neither Agree Nor Disagree	Somewhat Disagree	Disagree	Strongly Disagree	Not Applicable to Me
○	○	○	○	○	○	○	○

10. My employees regularly communicate with me about their job.

Strongly Agree	Agree	Somewhat Agree	Neither Agree Nor Disagree	Somewhat Disagree	Disagree	Strongly Disagree	Not Applicable to Me
○	○	○	○	○	○	○	○

11. I trust my employees.

Strongly Agree	Agree	Somewhat Agree	Neither Agree Nor Disagree	Somewhat Disagree	Disagree	Strongly Disagree	Not Applicable to Me
○	○	○	○	○	○	○	○

12. My employees have difficulty telling me the plain truth about work-related problems.

Strongly Agree	Agree	Somewhat Agree	Neither Agree Nor Disagree	Somewhat Disagree	Disagree	Strongly Disagree	Not Applicable to Me
○	○	○	○	○	○	○	○

13. My employees bring work-related problems to my attention quickly.

Strongly Agree	Agree	Somewhat Agree	Neither Agree Nor Disagree	Somewhat Disagree	Disagree	Strongly Disagree	Not Applicable to Me
○	○	○	○	○	○	○	○

14. My employees look at our organization as a high-performing team.

Strongly Agree	Agree	Somewhat Agree	Neither Agree Nor Disagree	Somewhat Disagree	Disagree	Strongly Disagree	Not Applicable to Me
○	○	○	○	○	○	○	○

15. When I make a work-related mistake, I discuss it with affected employees.

Strongly Agree	Agree	Somewhat Agree	Neither Agree Nor Disagree	Somewhat Disagree	Disagree	Strongly Disagree	Not Applicable to Me
○	○	○	○	○	○	○	○

16. Work-related performance problems among my employees are usually due to a lack of training.

Strongly Agree	Agree	Somewhat Agree	Neither Agree Nor Disagree	Somewhat Disagree	Disagree	Strongly Disagree	Not Applicable to Me
○	○	○	○	○	○	○	○

17. My employees tend to blame their work problems on others.

Strongly Agree	Agree	Somewhat Agree	Neither Agree Nor Disagree	Somewhat Disagree	Disagree	Strongly Disagree	Not Applicable to Me
○	○	○	○	○	○	○	○

18. I spend too much time going over the same messages and directions to my employees.

Strongly Agree	Agree	Somewhat Agree	Neither Agree Nor Disagree	Somewhat Disagree	Disagree	Strongly Disagree	Not Applicable to Me
○	○	○	○	○	○	○	○

19. Lack of information accounts for important work-related problems involving my employees.

Strongly Agree	Agree	Somewhat Agree	Neither Agree Nor Disagree	Somewhat Disagree	Disagree	Strongly Disagree	Not Applicable to Me
○	○	○	○	○	○	○	○

20. I believe my employees would rate their working relationship with me very positively.

Strongly Agree	Agree	Somewhat Agree	Neither Agree Nor Disagree	Somewhat Disagree	Disagree	Strongly Disagree	Not Applicable to Me
○	○	○	○	○	○	○	○

Manager to Senior Leadership Survey

1. I speak up to provide senior leaders with the information they need to do their jobs well.

Strongly Agree	Agree	Somewhat Agree	Neither Agree Nor Disagree	Somewhat Disagree	Disagree	Strongly Disagree	Not Applicable to Me
○	○	○	○	○	○	○	○

2. I communicate truthfully with senior leaders in my written, oral, and online messages.

Strongly Agree	Agree	Somewhat Agree	Neither Agree Nor Disagree	Somewhat Disagree	Disagree	Strongly Disagree	Not Applicable to Me
○	○	○	○	○	○	○	○

3. Senior leaders must often read between the lines to understand what I really mean in my communications.

Strongly Agree	Agree	Somewhat Agree	Neither Agree Nor Disagree	Somewhat Disagree	Disagree	Strongly Disagree	Not Applicable to Me
○	○	○	○	○	○	○	○

4. There is much that I am not telling senior leaders about their leadership skills.

Strongly Agree	Agree	Somewhat Agree	Neither Agree Nor Disagree	Somewhat Disagree	Disagree	Strongly Disagree	Not Applicable to Me
○	○	○	○	○	○	○	○

5. I tend to make up stories or excuses for work-related problems.

Strongly Agree	Agree	Somewhat Agree	Neither Agree Nor Disagree	Somewhat Disagree	Disagree	Strongly Disagree	Not Applicable to Me
○	○	○	○	○	○	○	○

6. I openly discuss with senior leaders my opinions, observations, and suggestions.

Strongly Agree	Agree	Somewhat Agree	Neither Agree Nor Disagree	Somewhat Disagree	Disagree	Strongly Disagree	Not Applicable to Me
○	○	○	○	○	○	○	○

7. I trust the company's senior leaders.

Strongly Agree	Agree	Somewhat Agree	Neither Agree Nor Disagree	Somewhat Disagree	Disagree	Strongly Disagree	Not Applicable to Me
○	○	○	○	○	○	○	○

8. Senior leaders make sure to discuss difficult work-related issues with me.

Strongly Agree	Agree	Somewhat Agree	Neither Agree Nor Disagree	Somewhat Disagree	Disagree	Strongly Disagree	Not Applicable to Me
○	○	○	○	○	○	○	○

9. I discuss my opinions and concerns with senior leaders about the company and its business direction.

Strongly Agree	Agree	Somewhat Agree	Neither Agree Nor Disagree	Somewhat Disagree	Disagree	Strongly Disagree	Not Applicable to Me
○	○	○	○	○	○	○	○

10. I regularly communicate with senior leaders about my job.

Strongly Agree	Agree	Somewhat Agree	Neither Agree Nor Disagree	Somewhat Disagree	Disagree	Strongly Disagree	Not Applicable to Me
○	○	○	○	○	○	○	○

11. The company's senior leaders trust me.

Strongly Agree	Agree	Somewhat Agree	Neither Agree Nor Disagree	Somewhat Disagree	Disagree	Strongly Disagree	Not Applicable to Me
○	○	○	○	○	○	○	○

12. I have difficulty telling senior leaders the plain truth about work-related problems.

Strongly Agree	Agree	Somewhat Agree	Neither Agree Nor Disagree	Somewhat Disagree	Disagree	Strongly Disagree	Not Applicable to Me
○	○	○	○	○	○	○	○

13. I bring work-related problems to senior leaders' attention quickly.

Strongly Agree	Agree	Somewhat Agree	Neither Agree Nor Disagree	Somewhat Disagree	Disagree	Strongly Disagree	Not Applicable to Me
○	○	○	○	○	○	○	○

14. I look at our organization as a high-performing team.

Strongly Agree	Agree	Somewhat Agree	Neither Agree Nor Disagree	Somewhat Disagree	Disagree	Strongly Disagree	Not Applicable to Me
○	○	○	○	○	○	○	○

15. When the company's senior leaders make a work-related mistake, they discuss it with affected employees.

Strongly Agree	Agree	Somewhat Agree	Neither Agree Nor Disagree	Somewhat Disagree	Disagree	Strongly Disagree	Not Applicable to Me
○	○	○	○	○	○	○	○

16. Work-related performance problems I experience are usually due to a lack of training.

Strongly Agree	Agree	Somewhat Agree	Neither Agree Nor Disagree	Somewhat Disagree	Disagree	Strongly Disagree	Not Applicable to Me
○	○	○	○	○	○	○	○

17. I tend to blame my own work problems on others.

Strongly Agree	Agree	Somewhat Agree	Neither Agree Nor Disagree	Somewhat Disagree	Disagree	Strongly Disagree	Not Applicable to Me
○	○	○	○	○	○	○	○

18. Senior leaders spend too much time going over the same messages and directions to managers.

Strongly Agree	Agree	Somewhat Agree	Neither Agree Nor Disagree	Somewhat Disagree	Disagree	Strongly Disagree	Not Applicable to Me
○	○	○	○	○	○	○	○

19. Lack of information accounts for important work-related problems I encounter on the job.

Strongly Agree	Agree	Somewhat Agree	Neither Agree Nor Disagree	Somewhat Disagree	Disagree	Strongly Disagree	Not Applicable to Me
○	○	○	○	○	○	○	○

20. I rate my working relationship with the company's senior leaders very positively.

Strongly Agree	Agree	Somewhat Agree	Neither Agree Nor Disagree	Somewhat Disagree	Disagree	Strongly Disagree	Not Applicable to Me
○	○	○	○	○	○	○	○

Guide for Workers to Evaluate Workplace Trust

We've all heard the expression, "Take it with a grain of salt." In other words, don't trust everything you hear. One way to measure a person's trustworthiness in your professional life is to decide how many grains of salt you have to take while listening to him or her. Here's a handy guide to gauging trust among your coworkers.

Grains of Salt	Coworker
0 Grains	It's hard to believe you found a coworker to work with and rely on who is as trustworthy as your mother.
1 Grain	Trust but verify. Work hard and well with this coworker but keep your eyes and ears open.
2 Grains	Independently corroborate all assertions. Make sure everything that matters is in writing even if it's just email.
3 Grains	Only work with this coworker if you have no alternative.
4 Grains	Do not walk. Run from this company if they keep workers like this on the payroll.

Management

You are one of the very fortunate workers who has a boss who cares about you and your work. Make this boss your mentor.

Spot-check the one-grainers for possible omissions, delays, or sugarcoating of information.

Corroborate assertions that affect you, your job, and your work group. Check constantly for omissions, sugarcoating, and fabricating of key information.

Clean up the resume for another job within your company or look outside for a new job.

Your mortgage payment, children's tuition bills, or proximity to retirement compel you to work here.

Business-to-Business

Adopt this supplier or vendor as your child.

Regularly check for quality issues, on-schedule deliveries, cost overruns, and price increases.

Put all specs and purchasing details (especially delivery dates) in writing, especially if purchasing a mission-critical product or service. Include enforceable penalties for late or partial performance.

You are obviously working with this supplier because of price, convenience, or only source for a key component or service.

Have your lawyer call their lawyer.

Chapter Eleven

Conclusion

"Our market system depends critically on trust—trust in the word of our colleagues and trust in the word of those with whom we do business."
Alan Greenspan

We believe that clearly identifiable yet rarely discussed factors in American businesses are frustrating employees, slowing productivity, and stifling innovation. The single umbrella phrase for these negative forces is "lack of trust." When bosses don't trust employees, morale suffers, worker motivation crashes, and employee and business performance plummets. When employees don't trust bosses, leadership falters. When employees don't trust one another, teamwork becomes just an idea in a Human Resources manual. In a larger sphere, when customers don't trust companies, no amount of catchy marketing or price cuts can sustain a client base.

In this book, we welcomed back key words and concepts that have not been used lately when business leaders try to figure out what's going on, and what's not, in their companies. Take "candor," for example. It is unlikely that the word or idea appears as a category on any employee's performance evaluation form, yet what wouldn't business leaders give for basic candor from their employees: telling it like it is instead of spinning, obscuring, or silencing the message. And what wouldn't employees give for basic candor from their bosses—an end to management by mystery—and in its place open and frank discussions of business issues.

In this book, we point out the price paid by business when a lack of candor destroys trust. In the case of the employee's late report assignment, the boss goes chasing after claimed failures in IT service ("the network was down") or the communication system ("I didn't get the memo") only to finally conclude that he is managing a liar. As in the case of Vic in Chapter Six, more than one professional has left home in the morning as an honest, plain-spoken father, husband, or partner only to metamorphose at work into a deceptive manipulator of people and information.

We ask readers to imagine, by contrast, a workplace where genuine candor is the norm and standard, not the nostalgic memory. We cling to the idea that candor is a freeing force in business in that it allows plans to be made based on how things actually are rather than on a hyped, twisted version of reality created to save face, dodge work, or play office politics. What finer statement could a boss make about an employee than, "I can count on her to tell it like it is." And, conversely, what employee wouldn't yearn to say with conviction, "My boss would never deceive me."

Out of relationships characterized by candor emerges trust. At heart, this book endeavors to clear a path long overgrown and obscured due to lack of use. We guide company leaders, employees, and general business to take four crucial steps on the way to individual and organizational success:

- Realize the importance of trust not only for human relationships in the workplace, but for what those working relationships are supposed to *produce*: valued products and services, bright ideas for the future, an expanding base of delighted customers, and an ever-improving bottom line.
- Look in the mirror to evaluate your own relationship to trust. Where do you stand on core issues of personal integrity? How do you handle daily pressures to make up excuses, blame others unfairly, or put yourself in

a better light than you deserve? Have you lost the vision of honest people working together for honorable ends?
- Evaluate the health of trust throughout your business. Does your organization impede or foster the exchange of information and ideas within the workforce? Is your company structured to make sure that people and knowledge are easily accessible? Do managers trust the top leaders? Do managers trust each another? Do employees trust their managers? Do employees even trust one another?
- Understand what lies beneath the symptoms of distrust, determining specific ways to rebuild trust within your work group, department, division, or company. So your company has a trust problem. You're hardly alone. Do you understand the roots of distrust in your company (or within yourself)? In this book, we don't buy the "bad people" explanation for a pervasive lack of trust within companies. Granted that people are not perfect, we concur with Douglas MacGregor in his classic description of Theory Y managers and employees, namely, those who, given the chance, will give their best effort willingly and often with pleasure; who will speak with candor at work because they respect one another; who trust that their work is valued; and who receive the trust of those who employ them.

We also need to set aside a few false notions, in effect, what this book is *not* about. First, we aren't wearing rose-colored glasses in our view of American workers and their companies. We recognize that some individuals and companies are untrustworthy to their core, deeply ingrained with habits of deceit in their statements, deception in their relationships, and corruption in their business practices. We admit that deceptive business people often make a lot of money—more, at times, than trustworthy competitors who are striving to uphold company values that are good for their clients, community, country, and planet. But few would disagree that over time the stench of deceit drives away employees and customers. Truly sustainable businesses look at renewable physical resources and at nurturing and rewarding the motivation, creativity, collaboration and trust of their employees. Trust sustains businesses. Lack of trust inevitably destroys businesses.

Second, we aren't interested here in naming names of CEOs and other business leaders who have made themselves notorious for a lack of candor, making them widely distrusted (and sometimes jailed). Their stories have received more than ample coverage in newspapers, magazines, TV, and radio. Highlighting them yet again would give the false impression that leadership alone, whether decent or deceitful, is the arena where the battle for trust is won or lost. Not so. While a leader can often set the tone for trust or distrust in an organization, he or she does not play the entire symphony. Trust, if it is to be a key player and contributor in company success, must become the default mode for all company communications and relationships, the standard operating procedure, the only practice because it is the best practice.

Third, we will be the first to agree that many factors beyond those treated in this book combine to produce a successful company. Whole bookshelves are filled with advice on everything from financial strategies to personnel policies to marketing techniques. We want to write what's not on that shelf: the case for basic candor leading to individual and organizational trust. And that trust, we argue, is not simply a desirable human end in itself, but is a potent factor—perhaps the most potent factor—in determining which companies succeed and which fail. Trust, in other words, isn't a "soft" agenda item, restricted only to how employees should relate in an ideal world. Trust is as "hard" a priority as the balance sheet itself and especially influential on the bottom line. (Ironically, the level of trustworthiness within a company determines whether we can even believe the balance sheet.)

Finally, we agree that trust, like all human relationships, is complex and highly situational. It would be foolhardy to trust everyone. It would be equally quixotic, no matter what our ideals for ourselves, to claim that we are trustworthy at all times and in all circumstances. There are inevitable sticking points in any discussion of candor and trust: the dilemma of the boss who is bound to silence by the company with regard to impending layoffs but who nevertheless wants his employees to trust him; the quandary of the new employee who wants to speak her mind about obvious problems she observes in the workplace but bites her tongue out of fear of offending "the powers that be"; and the confusion of a manager who urges her employees, "Trust me," yet uses their candid disclosures to their disadvantage in terms of pay and promotion. This is all to say that trust fights for its existence in the midst of very human fears, ambitions, abilities, and frailties. But the fight is worth it!

Appendix A

Trust and Personality
A Diagnostic Instrument

When a coworker fails to communicate with candor, we would be mistaken in always chalking up that problem to stubbornness, dissembling, ill feelings, or other negative motives. Often we are simply experiencing "bad chemistry" with that person, in other words, a mismatch of personality types. The building of trust, after all, doesn't happen at the same pace or in the same ways with all people. Learning to recognize differences in personality types puts us a step ahead in working toward trust and candor with the various personalities we encounter in the workplace and beyond.

You may have noticed that you don't get along equally well with everyone you meet. That's hardly news for any of us. But you may have written off this common experience as "just a bad fit" or "not my cup of tea." Leaving personality connections in the mystery zone can put you behind in your professional and personal life. It is better to examine closely the distinct personality differences that can account for much miscommunication, including the awkward silences and lack of spontaneity that occur when people misunderstand or mistrust one another.

The following instrument helps you understand your own basic personality tendencies. With these in mind, you can easily determine with which other personality types you are likely to bond or to clash. Low levels of trust often occur when the communicating parties sense that they're just not on the same track. Left unattended, these misunderstandings can lead to a professional train wreck. The following short personality inventory can be your flashlight into the tunnel to at least spot the train and react accordingly before it reaches you.

The psychological theories of Swiss philosopher Carl Jung continue to provide an influential tool for interpersonal success in business. In 1921, Jung proposed the "type" theory, the idea that each of us is predisposed to certain personality tendencies. Jung arranged these qualities into four dimensions, with each dimension composed of opposite qualities. Some individuals, Jung said, are by nature more extroverted; some are more introverted. Some spend their energy handling details, while others work to grasp the big picture. Some operate predominantly by logic; some by emotion. Some are data gatherers, while others hurry on to conclusions. You need to know who you are in this scheme of personality definitions in order to predict and prepare for communicating candidly and productively with personalities quite unlike your own.

Here's how this evaluation works. You simply enter your *a* or *b* choices on the scorecard provided at the end of the list of questions. The interpretive guide accompanying the scorecard will help you understand your scores and make applications to the way you communicate with others in your business life.

Read each question and allow your gut response to guide your answer. In some cases, you may not have a strong preference, or neither of the answers seems to be right for you. In all cases, choose the answer that comes closest to your opinion. It may be most convenient to circle your answer for each question, then transfer your answers to the scorecard when you have completed the test.

1. In the workplace, you prefer to make social conversation with:
    a. many people during the day.
    b. only a few people during the day.
2. In learning a new work skill, you prefer to be trained by:
    a. following a step-by-step set of instructions.
    b. grasping the big picture and trying your own approach.
3. Your work associates value you most for what you:
    a. think (your rational abilities).
    b. feel (your "heart" or intuitions).
4. As you review major accomplishments by others in your industry, you believe their achievements have been due to:
    a. pushing hard to make things happen.
    b. looking beyond obvious answers for new possibilities.
5. In your work relationships, you consider yourself popular with:
    a. many people.
    b. only a few people.
6. In considering a job change, you would prefer to hear about:
    a. what employees at a new company are doing.
    b. how employees at the new company are being prepared for future challenges.
7. When a new worker enters your work environment, you form impressions based on:
    a. their appearance and actions.
    b. the way they make you feel when you are with them.
8. In making business purchases, you select items:
    a. quickly, because you know what you want.
    b. after careful comparison shopping.
9. At work you prefer jobs that bring you in contact with:
    a. many people during the day.
    b. few if any people during the day.
10. When you have too much to do in your day, you respond by:
    a. finding extra energy to meet the challenges.
    b. stopping to revise your plans and schedules.

11. In managing others, it would be most important for you to be:
    a. logical.
    b. friendly.
12. In arranging business deals, you:
    a. save time for all concerned by spelling out the major points of agreement and leaving minor points to good faith between the parties.
    b. spell out both major and minor details, even if such work takes extra time.
13. At work you consider yourself to have:
    a. many friends.
    b. few if any friends.
14. You think a company leader should be:
    a. informative.
    b. organized.
15. When a coworker confides in you about a personal problem, you:
    a. try to offer a possible solution.
    b. feel and express sympathy.
16. In superior-subordinate relationships at work, you believe duties between the parties should be:
    a. stated clearly in written or spoken form.
    b. left open to allow for flexibility and new opportunities.
17. When meeting a new employee, you:
    a. take the initiative in showing warmth and friendliness
    b. wait for him or her to show signs of friendliness.
18. You believe children be raised to:
    a. learn real-world skills and behaviors as soon as they are ready.
    b. set goals and stick to their commitments.
19. In work relationships, it is more dangerous to show:
    a. too much emotion and personality.
    b. too little emotion and personality.

Trust and Personality: A Diagnostic Instrument 207

20. In designing interview questions for use in hiring a manager, you create:
    a. questions with definite answers.
    b. questions that are open-ended.
21. An old acquaintance (but not a good friend) unexpectedly encounters you in the lobby of a convention hotel. You tend to find this chance meeting:
    a. enjoyable.
    b. somewhat uncomfortable.
22. In choosing artwork to hang on company walls, you choose paintings that:
    a. are quite different from one another.
    b. work together to communicate a single theme or impression.
23. In deciding which candidate to support for a leadership position in your company, you favor:
    a. an intelligent, cool-headed candidate.
    b. a passionate and well-intentioned candidate.
24. You prefer social get-togethers that are:
    a. carefully planned.
    b. largely unplanned.
25. In going out to lunch with coworkers, you prefer to be with:
    a. many coworkers.
    b. one or two coworkers.
26. You believe that presidents of companies should have:
    a. excellent skills.
    b. well-developed plans.
27. You are passing through a city on business and want to stop by to say hello to a former colleague who lives there. You:
    a. make specific time and place arrangements with the person well in advance of your trip.
    b. give the person a pleasant surprise by a call out of the blue.

28. When attending a company social event taking place at 8 PM, you:
    a. arrive right on time.
    b. arrive somewhat late.
29. In making business phone calls, you:
    a. make the most of the conversation, allowing little time for the other person to speak.
    b. spend most of your time listening and commenting briefly on what the other person is saying.
30. In moments of leisure, you read:
    a. a letter to the editor in a news magazine.
    b. an article about city planning.
31. In choosing movies, you tend to select those that:
    a. explain social conditions and historical periods.
    b. produce laughter or tears.
32. In preparing to be interviewed for a job, you prepare to talk more about:
    a. achievements.
    b. future goals and plans.
33. If forced to accept dormitory accommodations during a conference, you prefer to stay in a room:
    a. with a few other compatible conference participants.
    b. alone.
34. In making work decisions, you are most influenced by:
    a. the facts of the situation at hand.
    b. the implications of the situation at hand.
35. In hiring employees to work for you, they should be primarily:
    a. intelligent and wise.
    b. loyal and hardworking.
36. In purchasing real estate, it is more important to:
    a. be ready to snap up a good deal before it disappears.
    b. have thorough knowledge of available properties.
37. In making a consumer complaint, you prefer to:
    a. call the company and talk to a customer representative.
    b. write to the company.

38. When performing an ordinary work task, you prefer to:
    a. do whatever works.
    b. do what is usually done.
39. In court, judges should:
    a. follow the letter of the law.
    b. show leniency or strictness where they think it appropriate.
40. When given a project to complete, you prefer someone to give you:
    a. a deadline.
    b. the freedom to turn the project in when you feel it is ready.
41. When introducing two work associates who do not know each other, you tend to:
    a. tell them each a bit of information about the other to facilitate conversation.
    b. let them make their own conversation.
42. It is worse for a manager to be too:
    a. idealistic.
    b. flexible.
43. When you listen to a business presentation, you prefer a speaker who:
    a. proves his or her points with data and specific examples.
    b. communicates excitement and deep commitment for the topic.
44. At the end of the work day, you spend more time thinking about what you:
    a. did during the day.
    b. are going to do the next day.
45. In planning your ideal vacation, you choose a place where you can:
    a. meet with family and friends.
    b. be alone or with only one to two family members or friends.

46. At work, you prefer to:
    a. meet deadlines.
    b. predict coming events.
47. If you were president of a company, it would be more important to you that all employees:
    a. understand their job responsibilities thoroughly.
    b. feel part of the company family.
48. As a member of a project team, you prefer to be most involved in:
    a. the completion stage in which final details are wrapped up.
    b. the initial conceptualization stage in which approaches are debated.
49. When learning new skills, you prefer to be taught:
    a. as part of a small class.
    b. one on one by a trainer.
50. If you had just two novels to choose between for leisure reading, you would be more likely to select:
    a. a realistic novel about people and places.
    b. a mystery novel at the end of which everything becomes clear.
51. When you consider your career path, you believe you should:
    a. plan career moves months or years in advance.
    b. follow your heart as opportunities arise.
52. In paying tribute to a retiring company leader, you focus primarily on the person's:
    a. achievements.
    b. aspirations.
53. You think the main purpose of business meetings is:
    a. getting to know one another and building team spirit.
    b. getting work done as efficiently as possible.
54. You are most adept at:
    a. drawing conclusions from facts.
    b. raising long-term questions and issues.

55. The most important quality a workforce can have is:
    a. up-to-date education.
    b. team spirit.
56. Which of the following words comes closest to describing your behavior at work?
    a. Impatient
    b. Curious
57. If your employer wanted to honor you at a luncheon, you would prefer a luncheon attended by:
    a. many company employees.
    b. your employer and one or two others.
58. In general, highly successful companies need:
    a. common sense.
    b. foresight.
59. Which of these two things would be better to say about a retiring employee?
    a. He or she was smart at his or her job.
    b. He or she cared deeply about coworkers.
60. In working on a team project, you:
    a. move it along to completion before the due date.
    b. make sure team members have considered all relevant information.

Scorecard

Transfer your answers as a check in the appropriate spaces below.

1. a___ b___	2. a___ b___	3. a___ b___	4. a___ b___
5. a___ b___	6. a___ b___	7. a___ b___	8. a___ b___
9. a___ b___	10. a___ b___	11. a___ b___	12. a___ b___
13. a___ b___	14. a___ b___	15. a___ b___	16. a___ b___
17. a___ b___	18. a___ b___	19. a___ b___	20. a___ b___
21. a___ b___	22. a___ b___	23. a___ b___	24. a___ b___
25. a___ b___	26. a___ b___	27. a___ b___	28. a___ b___
29. a___ b___	30. a___ b___	31. a___ b___	32. a___ b___
33. a___ b___	34. a___ b___	35. a___ b___	36. a___ b___
37. a___ b___	38. a___ b___	39. a___ b___	40. a___ b___
41. a___ b___	42. a___ b___	43. a___ b___	44. a___ b___
45. a___ b___	46. a___ b___	47. a___ b___	48. a___ b___
49. a___ b___	50. a___ b___	51. a___ b___	52. a___ b___
53. a___ b___	54. a___ b___	55. a___ b___	56. a___ b___
57. a___ b___	58. a___ b___	59. a___ b___	60. a___ b___
___ ___	___ ___	___ ___	___ ___
M S	J P	T E	C R

Add up the total number of checks for the *a* and *b* columns. For each pair of letters at the bottom of the columns, circle the letter for the column containing more checks. You should circle four letters altogether. The letters refer to the eight personality descriptions presented below. The higher the number of checks, the more dominant that characteristic is in your personality.

Why four dominant traits? None of us consistently acts in accordance with only one personality characteristic. Instead, various traits (such as those you've identified by the letters you've circled) interact, often in unpredictable ways, to produce the whole personality known as "you." Let's say, for example, that your score identifies you as an MJEC, with dominant traits in the Member, Juggler, Empathizer, and Closer categories. Read through the descriptions of these personality types and reflect upon how those traits interact in your personality. Perhaps in times of stress, one or more traits come to the fore. Perhaps some traits are more evident at home while others are dominant at work.

Personality Characteristics That Influence Candor in Communication

M—Member
This personality trait predisposes you to enjoy and seek out the company of others. The Member joins groups willingly, finds ways to include others in activities, and may tend to avoid tasks that must be accomplished alone. The Member relies on the consensus of the group for important decisions and may hesitate to form or express personal opinions without having them validated first by the group. The Member derives emotional support and strength from belonging, popularity, and having the respect of others.

In communicating, the Member may have a tendency to say what the group wants to hear and to shy away from messages that will be unpopular with the group. The Member will probably build alliances with those who can be trusted not to speak out of turn in ways that will distress the group. Conversely, the Member may not be supportive of anyone who is a loose cannon and whose words and opinions may fly counter to the dominant beliefs and feelings of the group.

S—Self
This personality trait predisposes you to individual initiation and solitary work habits. The Self joins groups only for a compelling reason, and even then only for the period of the task at hand. The Self looks with suspicion upon widely held opinions and groupthink. When faced by tasks too extensive or difficult for a single person to accomplish, the Self opts to divide work

tasks into portions that can be managed by several individuals working alone. The Self derives emotional support and strength from measuring up to personal standards, not the judgment of others.

In communicating, the Self will tend to tell it like it is without much regard for the feelings of others. To the Self, being right is more important than being liked. The Self often inadvertently sabotages the success of messages by not weighing their social impact and consequences. "She's probably right," a coworker may say of a Self communicator, "but it's the way she says things that make me really dislike her."

J—Juggler

This personality trait predisposes you to minute-by-minute, seemingly practical adjustments to changing conditions. The Juggler manages to keep many tasks in progress at once, all in a partial state of completion. The panic of impending deadlines and the unpredictability of interruptions and emergencies are all energizing and challenging for the Juggler. It is a matter of pride to the Juggler that he or she can handle situations, cope, and eventually see projects through to fulfillment. The Juggler derives emotional support and strength from a sense of sustained busyness as well as a conviction of his or her specialness and value to the group.

In communicating, the Juggler may tend to say anything in an effort to meet the emergency of the moment. Over time, the Juggler can acquire a reputation for lack of integrity because of this willingness to make up stories, excuses, and explanations as temporary bandages for this problem or that.

P—Planner

This personality trait predisposes you to place details, individual facts, and other data into patterns. The Planner then clings to these patterns tenaciously, for they serve to organize an otherwise bewildering array of discrete items. The Planner is resistant to receiving disorganized data before a plan has been developed; but after the planning stage, he or she welcomes information, particularly insofar as it supports the designated plan. The Planner derives emotional support and strength from a conviction of his or her usefulness as a shaping influence on disorderly projects and groups. To a degree, the Planner also derives emotional strength simply from the nature of the plan developed—its symmetry, scope, and interrelation of parts—no matter how events turn out.

In communicating, the Planner may tend to have a "prefix menu" in mind, no matter what the appetites of the audience at hand. If an hour-long PowerPoint presentation fits the plan of this personality type, he or she will press on with the presentation without regard for the interest, attention span, or stamina of the audience. In short, the Planner has difficulty adjusting his or her communication plan to the changing needs of the audience.

T—Thinker

This personality trait disposes you toward finding, or attempting to find, logical links between thoughts, ideas, concepts, facts, details, and examples. The Thinker insists on postponing action until he or she figures out the underlying causes, effects, and relative accuracy of propositions and assertions. When in a data-gathering mode, the Thinker is intent on knowing more; but when in assimilating and ratiocinating modes, the Thinker may reject or postpone new input of any kind. The Thinker derives emotional support and strength from the satisfaction of reaching logically defensible solutions to problems. Whether anyone acts on the basis of those solutions is less important to the Thinker than the success of the mental processes involved at arriving at them.

In communicating, the Thinker may arrange propositions in ways that are logically correct but interminably boring to the audience. "Why can't he just cut to the chase?" listeners may ask. For the Thinker, however, each and every step in the argument must be presented for the sake of intellectual completeness, no matter the bottom line communication needs and desires of the audience.

E—Empathizer

This personality trait predisposes you to focus on the emotional content of situations, as experienced personally or by others. The Empathizer appraises new information or a new situation first according to its emotional potential: How do I feel about this? How do others feel? Who will be hurt? Who will be happy? The answers to these questions play a prominent role in shaping the Empathizer's eventual point of view and action regarding the new information or situation. The Empathizer derives emotional support and strength from his or her self-image as a sensitive, caring individual and, often, from the gratitude and friendship of those targeted for his or her empathy.

In communicating, the Empathizer may provide more sustenance than substance in messages. Because the Empathizer wants to relate well on the level of mutual feelings, the message content may be distorted or sacrificed entirely for the sake of those feelings.

C—Closer

This personality trait predisposes you to make conclusions, judgments, and decisive acts, sometimes contrary to established procedures and rules. The Closer is generally impatient with delays urged by others for additional thought, research, or planning. The Closer often grants that the whole situation is not known but argues that enough of the factors or circumstances are already available for adequate decision making. This personality type can be deaf to input that does not contribute directly to finalizing projects and processes. The Closer derives emotional support and strength from his or her reputation in the group as an action-oriented, no-nonsense decision maker and from the satisfaction of having used power, tolerance for risk, and a measure of daring to manage difficult problems and personalities.

In communicating, the Closer may create statements that are falsely urgent or dramatic: "It's now or never," "We have a window of opportunity here that is going to close soon," "We could talk about this forever, but now's the time to act."

R—Researcher
This personality trait predisposes you to postpone judgment and action so long as it is possible to acquire new information. The Researcher craves certainty and suspects conclusions reached without consideration of all the evidence. The Researcher frequently ignores both time and resource constraints in pressing on with the search for additional data. In communicating that data to others, the Researcher may not be able to successfully organize and summarize the data gathered, since these activities both involve the drawing of tentative conclusions. The Researcher derives emotional support and strength from the treasure-hunt excitement of investigation, from the strong influence his or her findings have upon eventual planning, and from the admiration of the group for having such a knowledgeable individual as a team member.

In communicating, the Researcher may mine too deeply for his or her audience into abstruse questions and levels of detail. While such inquiries satisfy the nature of the Researcher, they lead many audience members to scream (if only internally), "Who cares?"

The implications of such personality information for communicators is clear: First, know your own communication tendencies so that you can be on guard against possible mismatches with your intended audience. Second, listen for the communication tendencies of others so that you can adapt to them for the purpose of achieving clear, efficient messaging. Finally, evaluate your own frustrations with the communications of others to determine if your feelings are coming from the fact that communication styles among individuals differ. You can reduce your frustrations significantly by taking proactive steps to adjust to those natural differences.

Appendix B

Recommended Readings

Ablow, Keith. *Living the Truth: Transform Your Life Through the Power of Insight and Honesty.* New York: Little, Brown, 2007.

Blackburn, Simon. *Truth: A Guide.* London: Oxford University Press, 2006.

Bok, Sissela. *Lying: Moral Choice in Public and Private Life.* New York: Vintage, 1999.

Bracey, Hyler. *Building Trust: How to Get It, How to Keep It.* New York: HB Artworks, 2003.

Covey, Stephen R., and Rebecca R. Merrill. *The Speed of Trust: One Thing That Changes Everything.* New York: Free Press, 2006.

Edelman, Ric. *The Lies about Money.* New York: Free Press, 2007.

Ford, Charles V. *Lies, Lies, Lies: The Psychology of Deceit.* New York: American Psychiatric Press, 1996.

Frankfurt, Harry G. *On Truth.* New York: Knopf, 2006.

Lieberman, David J. *Never Be Lied to Again.* New York: St. Martin's Griffin, 1999.

McClish, Mark. *I Know You Are Lying.* New York: Marpa Group, 2001.

Nance, Jef. *Conquering Deception.* New York: Irvin Benham Group, 2001.

Smith, David Livingston. *Why We Lie: The Evolutionary Roots of Deception and the Unconscious Mind.* New York: St. Martin's Griffin, 2007.

Thurman, Chris. *The Lies We Believe.* New York: Thomas Nelson, 2003.

Wall, Cynthia L. *The Courage to Trust: A Guide to Building Deep and Lasting Relationships.* Oakland, CA: New Harbinger, 2005.

Walters, Stanley B. The *Truth about Lying: How to Spot a Lie and Protect Yourself from Deception.* New York: Sourcebooks, 2000.